PENGUIN BOOKS

## ON DIRECTING FILM

Chicago-born David Mamet has written many plays, including *Glengarry Glen Ross*, for which he won both the Pulitzer Prize and the New York Drama Critics Circle Award, and most recently, *Oleana*. He is also the author of two collections of essays, *Writing in Restaurants* and *Some Freaks* (both Viking and Penguin), and has written and directed the movies *House of Games*, *Things Change*, and *Homocide*. He lives in Massachusetts and Vermont.

# ON

## DIRECTING

## FILM

### DAVID
### MAMET

PENGUIN BOOKS

PENGUIN BOOKS
Published by the Penguin Group
Penguin Books USA Inc.,
375 Hudson Street, New York, New York 10014, U.S.A.
Penguin Books Ltd, 27 Wrights Lane,
London W8 5TZ, England
Penguin Books Australia Ltd, Ringwood,
Victoria, Australia
Penguin Books Canada Ltd, 10 Alcorn Avenue,
Toronto, Ontario, Canada M4V 3B2
Penguin Books (N.Z.) Ltd, 182–190 Wairau Road,
Auckland 10, New Zealand

Penguin Books Ltd, Registered Offices:
Harmondsworth, Middlesex, England

First published in the United States of America by
Viking Penguin, a division of
Penguin Books USA Inc., 1991
Published in Penguin Books 1992

20

THE LIBRARY OF CONGRESS HAS CATALOGUED THE HARDCOVER AS FOLLOWS:
Mamet, David.
On directing film / David Mamet.
p.   cm.
ISBN 0–670–83033–X (hc.)
ISBN 0 14 01.2722 4 (pbk.)
1. Motion pictures — Production and direction.   I. Title.
PN1995.9.P7M28   1991
791.43′0233 — dc20        90–50428

Printed in the United States of America
Set in Perpetua
Designed by Fritz Metsch

THIS BOOK

IS DEDICATED TO

MIKE HAUSMAN.

They are most happy who have no
story to tell.

—Anthony Trollope,
*He Knew He Was Right*

I would like to thank my editor, Dawn Seferian, for her great patience; and Rachel Cline, Scott Zigler, Catherine Shaddix, and Elaine Goodall for their help in the construction of this book.

# PREFACE

This book is based on a series of lectures I gave at the film school of Columbia University in the fall of 1987.

The class was in Film Directing. I had just finished directing my second film, and like the pilot with two hundred hours of flying time, I was the most dangerous thing around. I had unquestionably progressed beyond the neophyte stage but was not experienced enough to realize the extent of my ignorance.

I offer the above in mitigation of a book on film directing written by a fellow with scant experience.

In support of the proposition, however, let me suggest this: that the Columbia lectures dealt with, and endeavored to explain, that theory of film directing I had concocted out of my rather more extensive experience as a screenwriter.

There was a newspaper review lately of a book about the career of a novelist who went to Hollywood and tried to succeed at writing screenplays. He was deluded, the reviewer said, in this pursuit—how could he have hoped to succeed as a screenwriter when he was nearly blind!

The reviewer exhibited a profound ignorance of the craft of screenwriting. One does not have to be able to see to write films; one has to be able to imagine.

There is a wonderful book called *The Profession of the Stage Director,* by Georgi Tovstonogov, who writes that a director may fall into one of the deepest pits by rushing immediately to visual or pictorial solutions.

This statement influenced and aided me greatly in my career as a stage director; and, subsequently, in my work as a screenwriter. If one understands *what the scene means,* and stages *that,* Mr. Tovstonogov was saying, one will be doing one's job for both the author and the viewer. If one rushes, first, into a pretty, or pictorial, or even descriptive staging, one may be hard-pressed to integrate that staging into the logical progression of the play. And, further, while so hard-pressed, and while working to include the pretty picture, one will undoubtedly become wedded to its eventual inclusion, to the detriment of the piece as a whole.

This concept was also stated by Hemingway as, "Write the story, take out all the good lines, and see if it still works."

My experience as a director, and as a dramatist, is this: the piece is moving in proportion to how much the author can leave out.

A good writer gets better only by learning to *cut,* to remove the ornamental, the descriptive, the narrative, and *especially* the deeply felt and meaningful. What remains? The story remains. What is the story? The story is the *essential progression of incidents* that occur to the hero in pursuit of his one goal.

The point, as Aristotle told us, is what happens to the *hero* . . . not what happens to the writer.

One does not have to be able to see to write such a story. One has to be able to think.

Screenwriting is a craft based on logic. It consists of the assiduous application of several very basic questions: What does the hero want? What hinders him from getting it? What happens if he does not get it?

If one follows the norms the application of those questions will create, one is left with a logical structure, an outline, from which outline the drama will be constructed. In a play, this outline is given to the other part of the dramatist—the ego of the structuralist hands the outline to the id, who will write the dialogue.

This conceit is analogous, I think, to the case of the structuralist screenwriter who gives the dramatic outline to the director.

I saw and see the director as that Dionysian extension of the screenwriter—who would finish the authorship in such a way that (as always should be the case) the drudgery of the technical work should be erased.

I came to film directing as a screenwriter, and saw the craft of directing as the joyful extension of screenwriting, and taught the class, and offer this book accordingly.

David Mamet
Cambridge, Massachusetts
Spring 1990

# ON

# DIRECTING

# FILM

# 1

# STORYTELLING

The main questions a director must answer are: "where do I put the camera?" and "what do I tell the actors?"; and a subsequent question, "what's the scene about?" There are two ways to approach this. Most American directors approach it by saying, "let's follow the actors around," as if the film were a record of what the protagonist did.

Now, if the film is a record of what the protagonist does, it had better be interesting. That is to say, this approach puts the director in a position of shooting the film in a novel way, an interesting way, and he or she is constantly wondering, "what's the most interesting place to put the camera to film this love scene? what's the most interesting way I can shoot it plainly? what's the most interesting way that I can allow the actor to behave in the scene in which, for example, *she proposes to him?*"

That's the way most American films are made, as a supposed record of what real people really did. There's another way to make a movie, which is the way that Eisenstein suggested a movie should be made. This method has nothing to do with following the protagonist around but rather is *a succession of images juxtaposed so that the contrast between these images moves the story forward in the mind of the audience.* This is a fairly succinct rendition of Eisenstein's theory of montage; it is also the first thing I know about film directing, virtually the *only* thing I know about film directing.

You always want to tell the story in cuts. Which is to say, through a juxtaposition of images that are basically uninflected. Mr. Eisenstein tells us that the best image is an uninflected image. A shot of a teacup. A shot of a spoon. A shot of a fork. A shot of a door. Let the cut tell the story. Because otherwise you have not got dramatic action, you have narration. If you slip into narration, you are saying, "you'll never guess why what I just told you is important to the story." It's unimportant that the audience should guess why it's important to the story. It's important simply to *tell* the story. Let the audience be surprised.

The movie, finally, is much closer than the play to simple storytelling. If you listen to the way people tell stories, you will hear that they tell them cinematically. They jump from one thing to the next, and the story is moved along by the juxtaposition of images—which is to say, by the *cut.*

People say, "I'm standing on the corner. It's a foggy day. A bunch of people are running around crazy. Might have been the full moon. All of a sudden, a car comes up and the guy next to me says . . ."

If you think about it, that's a shot list: (1) a guy standing on the corner; (2) shot of fog; (3) a full moon shining above; (4) a man says, "I think people get wacky this time of year"; (5) a car approaching.

This is good filmmaking, to juxtapose images. Now you're following the story. What, you wonder, is going to happen next?

The smallest unit is the shot; the largest unit is the film; and the unit with which the director most wants to concern himself is the scene.

First the shot: it's the juxtaposition of the shots that moves the film forward. The shots make up the scene. The scene is a formal essay. It is a small film. It is, one might say, a documentary.

Documentaries take basically unrelated footage and juxtapose it in order to give the viewer the idea the filmmaker wants to convey. They take footage of birds snapping a twig. They take footage of a fawn raising his head. The two shots have nothing to do with each other. They were shot days or years, and miles, apart. And the filmmaker juxtaposes the images to give the viewer the idea of *great alertness*. The shots have nothing to do with each other. They are not a record of what the protagonist did. They are not a record of how the deer reacted to the bird. They're basically uninflected images. But they give the viewer the idea of *alertness to danger* when they are juxtaposed. That's good filmmaking.

Now, directors should want to do the same thing. We should

all want to be documentary filmmakers. And we will have this advantage: we can go out and stage and film exactly those uninflected images we require for our story. And then juxtapose them. In the editing room, one is constantly thinking: "I wish I had a shot of . . ." Well, you've got all the time in the world before the film is shot: you can determine what shot you are going to require later, and go out and shoot it.

Almost no one in this country knows how to write a movie script. Almost all movie scripts contain material that cannot be filmed.

"Nick, a young fellow in his thirties with a flair for the unusual." You can't film it. How do you film it? "Jodie, a brash hipster, who's been sitting on the bench for thirty hours." How do you do that? It can't be done. Other than through narration (visual or verbal). Visual: Jodie looks at watch. Dissolve. It is now thirty hours later. Verbal: "Well, as hip as I am, it has surely been a trial to've been sitting on this bench for the last thirty hours." If you find that a point cannot be made without narration, it is virtually certain that the point is unimportant to the story (which is to say, to the audience): the audience requires not *information* but *drama*. Who, then, requires this *information?* This dreadful plodding narration that compromises almost all American filmscripts.

Most movie scripts were written for an audience of studio executives. Studio executives do not know how to read movie scripts. Not one of them. Not one of them knows how to read a movie script. A movie script should be a juxtaposition of uninflected shots that tell the story. To read this script and to "see" the movie will surely require either some cinematic education or some naïveté—neither of which is going to be found in the studio executive.

The work of the director is the work of constructing the shot list from the script. The work on the set is nothing. All you have to do on the set is stay awake, follow your plans, help the actors be simple, and keep your sense of humor. The film is directed in the making of the shot list. The work on the set is simply to record what has been chosen to be recorded. It is the *plan* that makes the movie.

I don't have any experience with film schools. I suspect that they're useless, because I've had experience with drama schools, and have found them to be useless.

Most drama schools teach things that will be learned by anyone in the normal course of events, and refrain from insulting the gentleman or gentlewoman student of liberal arts by offering instructions in a demonstrable skill. I suppose that film schools do the same. What should film schools teach? An understanding of the technique of juxtaposition of uninflected images to create in the mind of the viewer the progression of the story.

The Steadicam (a hand-held camera), like many another technological miracle, has done injury; it has injured American movies, because it makes it so easy to follow the protagonist around, one no longer has to think, "what is the shot?" or "where should I put the camera?" One thinks, instead, "I can shoot the whole thing in the morning." But if you love that morning's work at dailies (screenings of the footage you're shooting on a daily basis), you'll hate it when you're in the editing room. Because what you're seeing in dailies is not for your amusement; it should not be "little plays." It should be uninflected, short shots that can eventually cut, one to the other, to tell the story.

Here's why the images have to be uninflected. Two guys are walking down the street. One of them says to the other guy . . . Now you, reader, are listening: you are listening because you want to know *what happens next*. The shot list, and the work on the set, should be no more inflected than the cuts in the little story above. Two guys walking down the street . . . one guy starts to talk to the other . . .

*The purpose of technique is to free the unconscious.* If you follow the rules ploddingly, they will allow your unconscious to be free. That's true creativity. If not, you will be fettered by your conscious mind. Because the conscious mind always wants to be liked and wants to be interesting. The conscious mind is going to suggest the obvious, the cliché, because these things offer the security of having succeeded in the past. Only the mind that has been taken off itself and put on a task is allowed true creativity.

The mechanical working of the film is just like the mechanism of a dream; because that's what the film is really going to end up being, isn't it?

The images in a dream are vastly varied and magnificently interesting. And most of them are uninflected. It is their juxtaposition that gives the dream its strength. The terror and beauty of the dream come from the connection of previously unrelated mundanities of life. As discontinuous and as meaningless as that juxtaposition might seem on first glimpse, an enlightened analysis reveals the highest and the most simple order of organization and, so, the deepest meaning. Isn't that true?

The same should be true of a movie. The great movie can be as free of being a record of the progress of the protagonist as is a dream. I would suggest that those who are interested might want to do some reading in psychoanalysis, which is a great storehouse of information about movies. Both studies are basically the same. The dream and the film are the juxtaposition of images in order to answer a question.

I recommend, for example, *The Interpretation of Dreams* by Sigmund Freud; *The Uses of Enchantment* by Bruno Bettelheim; *Memories, Dreams, Reflections* by Carl Jung.

All film is, finally, a "dream sequence." How incredibly impressionistic even the worst, most plodding, most American movie is. *Platoon* really is not any more or less realistic than *Dumbo*. Both just happen to tell the story well, each in its own way. In other words, it's all make-believe. The question is, how *good* make-believe is it going to be?

# 2

# "WHERE DO YOU PUT

# THE CAMERA?"

## CONSTRUCTING A FILM
## (A COLLABORATION WITH
## STUDENTS IN THE COLUMBIA
## UNIVERSITY FILM SCHOOL)

MAMET:    Let's make a movie out of the situation we're in now. A bunch of people are coming to a class. What's an interesting way to film this?

STUDENT:  From above.

MAMET:    Now, why is that interesting?

STUDENT:  It's interesting because it's a novel angle and it gives a bird's-eye view of everybody coming in, sort of accentuating the numbers. If there are a number of people coming in, you may want to suggest that that's significant.

MAMET:    How can you tell if this is a good way to film the scene? There are any number of ways to film it. Why is "from above" better than any other angle?

How are you going to decide what's the best way to shoot it?

STUDENT: It depends what the scene is. You could say the scene is about a really tempestuous meeting and have people pacing around a lot. That would dictate a different scene than one in which the tension is underlying.

MAMET: That's exactly correct. You have to ask, "what is this scene about?" So let's put aside the "follow the hero around" way of making movies and ask what the scene is about. We have to say our task is *not* to follow the protagonist around. Why? Because there are an infinite number of ways to film a bunch of people in a room. So the scene is not simply about a bunch of people in a room; it's about something else. Let us suggest what the scene might be about. We know nothing about the scene other than it's a first meeting. So you're going to have to make an election as to what this scene is about. And it is this election, this choosing not "an interesting way" to film a scene (which is an election based on novelty and basically a desire to be well-liked) but rather saying, "I would like to make a statement based on the meaning of the scene, not the appearance of the scene," which is the choice of the artist. So let's suggest what the scene might be about. I'll give you a hint: "what does the protagonist want?" Because the scene ends when the protagonist gets it. What does the protagonist want? It's this journey that is going to move the story forward. What does the protagonist want? What does he or she do to get it—that's what keeps the audience in their seats. If you don't have that, you have to trick the audience into paying attention. Let's go back to the "class" idea. Let's say it's the first meeting of a series of people. A person, in the first meeting, might be trying to get respect. How are we going to address this subject cinematically? In this scene the subject wants *to earn the instructor's respect.* Let's tell the story in pictures. Now, if you have trouble addressing this thing, and your mind draws a blank, just listen to yourself telling the story to a guy next to you in a bar. How would you tell that story?

STUDENT:   "So this guy comes into the class and the first thing he does is sit right next to the professor and he started to look at him very carefully and . . . and listen very carefully to what he's saying and when the professor dropped his prosthetic arm, he reached down and grabbed it and gave it to the professor."

MAMET:   Well, yes. This is what the writers do today, the writers and directors. But we, on the other hand, want to keep everything that's "interesting" out of the way. If the character is not *made* to be interesting, then the character can only be interesting or un-interesting as it serves the story. It's impossible to make a character "interesting in general." If the story is about a man who wants to earn the respect of the instructor, it's not important that the instructor have a prosthetic arm. It's not our task to make the story interesting. The story can only be interesting because we find the progress of the protagonist interesting. It is the *objective of the protagonist* that keeps us in our seats. "Two small children went into a dark wood . . ." Okay; somebody else? You're writing the film. The objective is *to earn the respect of the instructor.*

STUDENT: "A guy in film class, who arrived twenty minutes early, sat at one end of the table. Then the class came in with the instructor, and he picked up his chair and moved it, trying to sit near the instructor, and the instructor sat on the other side of the room."

MAMET: Good. Now we've got some ideas. Let's work with them a little bit. A fellow arrived twenty minutes early. Why? *To earn the respect of his instructor.* He sat at one end of the table. Now, how can we reduce this to shots?

STUDENT: Shot of him coming in, shot of the classroom, shot of him sitting, shot of the rest of the class coming in.

MAMET: Good. Anybody else?

STUDENT: A shot of a clock, a shot of the moment when he comes in, hold on this until he decides where he's going to sit, a shot of him waiting alone in the empty room, a shot of the clock, and a shot of many people coming in.

MAMET: Do you need a shot of the clock? The smallest unit with which you most want to concern yourself is the shot. The larger concept of the scene is to win the respect of the instructor. This is what the protagonist wants—it's the superobjective. Now, how can we figure out the first beat of the scene? What do we do first?

STUDENT: Establish the character.

MAMET: The truth is, you never have to establish the character. In the first place, there is no such thing as character other than the habitual action, as Mr. Aristotle told us two thousand years ago. It just doesn't exist. Here or in Hollywood or otherwise. They always talk about the character out there in Hollywood, and the fact is there is no such thing. It doesn't exist. The character is just habitual action. "Character" is exactly what the person literally does in pursuit of the superobjective, the objective of the scene. The rest doesn't count.

An example: a fellow goes to a whorehouse and comes up to the madam and says, "what can I get for five bucks?" She says, "you should have been here yesterday, because . . ." Well, you, as members of the audience, want to know why he should have been there yesterday. That's what you want to know. Here, however, we tell the story, full of characterization.

A fellow, trim, fit, obviously enamored of the good  things of life but not without a certain somberness, which might speak of a disposition to contemplation, goes to a gingerbread gothic whorehouse situated on a quiet residential street, somewhere in a once-elegant part of town. While walking up the flagstone steps . . .

This is one of those American movies we make. The script and the film are always "establishing" something.

Now, don't *you* go "establishing" things. . Make the audience wonder what's going on *by putting them in the same position as the protagonist.*

As long as the protagonist wants something, the audience will want something. As long as the protagonist is clearly going out and attempting to get that something, the audience will wonder whether or not he's going to succeed. The moment the protagonist, or the *auteur* of the movie, stops trying to *get* something and starts trying to *influence* someone, the audience will go to sleep. The movie is not about establishing a character or a place, the way television does it.

Look at the story about the whorehouse: isn't that how most television shows are formed? A shot of "air," tilt down to frame a building. Pan down the building to a sign that says, "Elmville General Hospital." The point is not "where does the story take place?" but "what's it about?" That's what makes one movie different from another.

Let's go back to our movie. Now, what's the first concept? What is going to be a *building block that is necessary to "achieve the respect of the instructor"?*

STUDENT:    . . . The guy arrives early?

MAMET:      Exactly so. The guy arrives early. Now, the way you understand whether the concept is essential or not is to attempt to tell the story without it. Take it away and see if you need it or not. If it's not essential, you throw it out. Whether it's a scene or a shot, if it's not essential throw it out. "The guy says to the madam . . ." Well, obviously you can't start the whorehouse scene like that. You need something before that. "A guy goes to a whorehouse and the madam says . . ." In this example the first building block is "a guy goes to a whorehouse."

Here's another example: you have to walk to the elevator in order to get downstairs. In order to get down, you have to go to the elevator and get in there. That's essential to get downstairs. And if your objective is *to get to the subway* and you begin in an elevated floor of the building, the first step will be "to get downstairs."

*To win the respect of the instructor* is the superobjective. What steps are essential?

STUDENT:    First, *show up early*.

MAMET:      Good. Yes. How are we going to create this idea of earliness? We don't have to worry about *respect* now. *Respect* is the overall goal. All we have to worry about now is earliness; that's the first thing. So let's create the idea of earliness by juxtaposing uninflected images.

STUDENT:    He starts to sweat.

MAMET:      Okay, what are the images?

STUDENT:    The man sitting by himself, in a suit and tie, starting to sweat. You could watch his behavior.

MAMET:      How does this give us the idea of earliness?

STUDENT:    It would suggest that there's something he's anticipating.

MAMET:      No, we don't have to worry about anticipating. All we have to know in this beat is that he's early. Also, we don't have to watch behavior.

STUDENT:    An empty room.

MAMET:      Well, there we go, that's one image.

STUDENT:    A shot of a man by himself in an empty room juxtaposed with a shot of a group of people coming in from outside.

MAMET:      Okay, but this doesn't give us the idea of earliness, does it? Think about it.

STUDENT:    They could all be late.

MAMET:      Let's express this in absolutely pristine, uninflected images requiring no additional gloss. What are the two images that are going to give us the idea of *earliness*?

STUDENT:    A guy is walking down the street and the sun is rising and the street cleaners are going by and it's dawn and there's not a lot of activity on the street. And then maybe a couple of shots of some people waking up and then you see the guy, the first man, come into a room and other people are in there finishing up a job that they were doing, maybe finishing the ceiling or something like that.

MAMET: Now, this scenario gives the idea of early morning, but we've got to take a little bit of an overview. We have to let our little alarm go off once in a while, if we stray too far off the track; the alarm that says, "Yes—it's *interesting*, but does it fulfill the objective?" We want the idea of *earliness* so that we can use it as a building block to *winning respect*. We do not absolutely require the idea *early in the morning*.

STUDENT: Outside the door you could have a sign saying "Professor Such-and-such's class" and giving the time. Then you could have a shot of our guy obviously sitting by himself with the clock behind him.

MAMET: Okay. Does anybody feel that it might be a good idea to stay away from a clock? Why might we feel that?

STUDENT: Cliché.

MAMET: Yeah, it's a little bit of a cliché. Not that it's necessarily bad. As Stanislavsky told us, we shouldn't shy away from things just because they are clichés. On the other hand, maybe we can do better. Maybe the clock ain't bad, but let's put it aside for a moment just because our mind, that lazy dastard, jumped to it first and, perhaps, it is trying to betray us.

STUDENT: So you have him coming up, and he's in the elevator, nervous and maybe looking at his watch.

MAMET: No, no, no, no. We don't need this in there, do we? Why don't we need this?

STUDENT: Maybe a *small* clock . . . ?

MAMET:    . . . He doesn't even have to look nervous. This gets down to what I tell the actors too, which we'll discuss later. You can't rely on the acting to tell the story. He doesn't have to be nervous. The audience will get the idea. The *house* has to look like a house. The *nail* doesn't have to look like a house. This beat, as we described it, had nothing to do with "nervousness"; it is about *being early,* and that is *all* it is about. Now, what are the images here?

STUDENT:    We see the guy come down the hall and he gets to the door and is trying to rush in and he finds that it's locked. So he turns and looks for a janitor in the hall. The camera stays with him.

MAMET:    How do you know he's looking for a janitor? All you can do is take pictures. You can take a picture of a guy turning. You can't take a picture of a guy turning to look for a janitor. You've got to tell that in the next shot.

STUDENT:    Can you cut to a janitor?

MAMET:    Now the question is, does a shot of a guy turning and a shot of a janitor give you the idea of earliness? No, it doesn't. The important thing is *always apply the criteria.* This is the secret of filmmaking.

Alice said to the Cheshire Cat, "which road should I take?" And the Cheshire Cat said, "where do you want to go?" And Alice said, "I don't care." And the Cheshire Cat said, "then it doesn't matter which road you take." If, on the other hand, you *do* care where you're going, it does matter which road you take. All you have to think about now is *earliness*. Take a look at the idea about the locked door. How can we use this, because it's a very good idea. It's already more exciting than a clock. Not more exciting in general, but more exciting as applied to the idea of *earliness*.

STUDENT: He comes to the door and it's locked, so he turns, he sits and waits.

MAMET: Now, what are the shots? A shot of the man coming down a hall. What's the next shot?

STUDENT: A shot of a door, he tries it, it's locked, it doesn't open.

MAMET: He sits down?

STUDENT: That's it.

MAMET: Does this give us the idea of earliness? Yes?

STUDENT: What if we combine them all. Start with the sun rising. The second shot is of a janitor mopping in the hall, going down the hall, and as he goes down, there's someone sitting in front of the door and the guy gets up and points to the door and the janitor could look at his watch and the guy points to the door again and the janitor looks at his watch and shrugs and unlocks it.

MAMET: Which sounds cleaner? Which gives us more clarity in this instance? The toughest thing in writing and directing and editing is to give up preconceptions, and apply those tests you have elected are correct for the problem.

We do that by applying ourselves to our first

principles. The first principle, in this case of the scene, being it's not a scene about guys coming into a room, it's a scene about trying to win the respect of the instructor; the second small principle being this *beat* is about *earliness*. That's all we have to worry about, *earliness*.

Now, we have two plans here. Which is simpler? Always do things the least interesting way, and you make a better movie. This is my experience. Always do things the least interesting way, the most blunt way. Because then you will not stand the risk of falling afoul of the objective in the scene by being interesting, which will always bore the audience, who are collectively much smarter than you and me and have already gotten up to the punch line. How do we keep their attention? Certainly not by giving them *more* information but, on the contrary, by *withholding* information—by withholding *all* information except that information the absence of which would make the progress of the story incomprehensible.

This is the kiss rule. K.I.S.S. Keep it simple, stupid. So we have three shots. A fellow is walking down the hall. Tries the handle of the door. Close-up of the door handle being jiggled. Then the fellow sits down.

STUDENT:     I think you need one more shot if you want to show his earliness. He opens up his briefcase, pulls out a handful of pencils, and starts sharpening them.

MAMET:  Okay now, you're getting ahead of yourself. We've finished our task, right? Our task is done when we've established the idea of earliness.

As William of Occam told us, when we have two theories, each of which adequately describes a phenomenon, always pick the simpler. Which is a different way of keeping it simple, stupid. Now, you don't eat a whole turkey, right? You take off the drumstick and you take a bite of the drumstick. Okay. Eventually you get the whole turkey done. It'll probably get dry before you do, unless you have an incredibly good refrigerator and a very small turkey, but that is outside the scope of this lecture.

So we've taken the drumstick off the turkey— the turkey being the scene. We've taken a bite off the drumstick, the bite being the specific beat of *earliness*.

So let us posit the identity of the second beat. We don't have to follow the protagonist around, do we? What's the next question we have to ask?

STUDENT:  What's the next beat?

MAMET:  Exactly so. What's the next beat? Now, we have something we can compare this next beat to, don't we?

STUDENT:  The first beat.

MAMET:  Something else, which will help us to figure out what it's going to be. What is it?

STUDENT:  The scene?

MAMET:  The *objective* of the scene: exactly. The question the answer to which will unerringly guide us is, "what's the objective of the scene?"

STUDENT: Respect.

MAMET: *To win the respect of the instructor* is the overall objective of the scene. That being the case, if we know the first thing is *to arrive early,* what might be a second thing? A *positive* and essential second beat, having arrived early. In order to do what . . . ?

STUDENT: To earn the respect of the instructor.

MAMET: Yes. So what might one do? Or another way to ask it is why did he arrive early? We know *to win the respect of the instructor* is the superobjective.

STUDENT: He might get out the instructor's book and brush up on the instructor's methodology.

MAMET: No. That's too abstract. You're on too high a level of abstraction. The first beat is *earliness.* So on the same level of abstraction, what might be the second beat? He was early in order to do what?

STUDENT: Prepare.

MAMET: Perhaps *in order to prepare.* Anyone else?

STUDENT: Now, don't we have to deal with the locked door? He has an obstacle: the door is locked; he has to respond to that obstacle.

MAMET: Forget about the protagonist. You have to know what the protagonist wants because that's what the film is about. But you don't have to take a picture of it. Hitchcock denigrated American films, saying they were all "pictures of people talking"—as, indeed, most of them are.

*You* tell the story. Don't let the protagonist tell the story. *You* tell the story; *you* direct it. We don't have to follow the protagonist around. We don't have to establish his "character." We don't need to have anybody's "back story." All we have to do is create an essay, just like a documentary; the subject of this particular documentary being *to win the respect of.* The first essay is on earliness; what's the second thing?

STUDENT:   Could it be *to wait?*

MAMET:    *To wait?* What's the difference between *to wait* and *to prepare?*

STUDENT:   The protagonist is more active.

MAMET:    In which?

STUDENT:   The second.

MAMET:    In terms of what?

STUDENT:   In terms of his action. It's stronger to have the actor *do* something.

MAMET:    I'll tell you a better test. *To prepare* is more active in terms of *this particular* superobjective. It's more active in terms of *to win the respect.*

This class is about one thing: learning to ask the question "what's it about?" The film is not about a guy. It's about *to win the respect of.* The beat is not about *a guy coming in.* It's about *earliness.* Now that we've taken care of earliness, let's say the next beat is *to prepare.* Tell the idea of *to prepare* as if you're telling it to somebody in a bar.

STUDENT:   So this guy was sitting on a bench waiting, waiting, just waiting. And he pulled out of his briefcase a book written by the professor.

MAMET: Now, how do you shoot that? How do you know it's a book written by the professor?

STUDENT: We could have the name of the professor on the door, and in the same shot see the name on the book.

MAMET: But we don't know that he's preparing for the class. You don't have to put in all this literary narration—see how narration weakens the film? You *do* have to know the beat is about *preparing*. It's a very important distinction. We don't have to know it's *preparing for the class*. That's going to take care of itself. We *do* have to know it's *preparing*. The boat has to look like a boat—the keel does not.

We don't need waiting. Waiting is trying to reiterate. We've already got *earliness*. We took care of that. All we have to do now is *preparing*. Listen to yourselves when you describe these shots. When you use the words "just," "kind of," and "sort of," you're diluting the story. The shots shouldn't be just, kind of, or sort of anything. They should be straightforward, as straightforward as the first three shots in the movie.

STUDENT: He starts to comb his hair, straighten his tie.

MAMET: Does this fall under the heading of *preparing*?

STUDENT: It's like *grooming*.

MAMET: Preparing could be preparing *physically* or it could be preparing for the subject matter at hand—*to win the respect of.*

Which is going to be more specific to the scene? What is going to be more specific to the overall superobjective, *to win the respect of the instructor?* To make oneself more attractive, or to prepare?

STUDENT: He pulls out his notebook, reads through it very fast, then thinks, no, then he goes back and looks at a certain page.

MAMET: Now, this falls afoul of one of the precepts we have been discussing, which is: tell the story in *cuts.* We're going to adopt this as our motto.

Obviously there are some times when you are going to need to follow the protagonist around for a bit; but only when that is the best way to tell the story; which, if we are dedicated in the happy application of these criteria, we will find is very seldom the case. See, while we have the luxury of time, here in class or at home making up the storyboard, we have the capacity to tell the story the best way. We can then go on the set and film it.

When we're on the set, we don't have this luxury. Then we *have* to follow the protagonist around, and we'd better have ourselves a Steadicam.*

---

*The Steadicam is no more capable of aiding in the creation of a good movie than the computer is in the writing of a good novel—both are labor-saving devices, which simplify and so make more attractive the mindless aspects of a creative endeavor.

So what we're trying to do is find two or more shots the juxtaposition of which will give us the idea of *preparing*.

STUDENT: How about: this guy has a three-ring binder. And he takes a little piece of white cardboard and rips off the perforated edges, folds them in half, puts them into the little plastic tabs that divide the pages in the three-ring binder.

MAMET: This is an interesting idea. Let's say it in shots: he takes his notebook, he takes out a piece of paper, which is one of those little tabs. We cut to the insert (a tight shot on his hands). He's writing something on the tab. He sticks the piece of paper in the plastic thing. Now we cut back out to the master (the main shot of the scene). He closes the notebook. This is all uninflected, isn't it? Does this give us the idea of *preparing?* I'll ask you another question: which is more interesting—if we read what he's writing on the tab or if we *don't* read what he's writing?

STUDENT: If we don't.

MAMET: Exactly so. It's much more interesting if we don't read what he's writing. Because if we read what he's writing, then the sneaky purpose of the scene becomes *to narrate*, doesn't it? It becomes to tell the audience where we are. If we don't have any sneaky purpose in the scene, then all that beat has to be about is *preparation*. What's the effect of this on the audience?

STUDENT:     It arouses their curiosity.

MAMET:       Exactly so, and it also wins their respect and thanks, because we have treated *them* with respect, and have not exposed them to the unessential. We want to know what he's writing. It's obvious that he was *early*. It's obvious that he is *preparing*. We want to know: early for what? preparing for what? Now we've put the audience in the same position as the protagonist. *He's* anxious to do something and *we're* anxious for him to do something, right? So we're telling the story very well. It's a good idea. I have another idea, but I think yours is better.

My idea is that he shoots his cuffs and that he looks down at his cuff, and we cut to an insert and we see the shirt has still got the tag on it. So he rips the tag off. No, I think yours is better, because it goes more to the idea of *preparedness*. Mine was kind of cute, but yours has much more to do with preparedness. If you have the time, as we do now, you compare your idea to the objective, and as the good philosophers we are, as followers of the ways of both the Pen and the Sword, we choose the way that is closer to the objective, discarding that which is merely cute or interesting; and *certainly* discarding that which has a "deep personal meaning" for us.

If you're out on the set, and you don't have any leisure at all, you may choose something simply because it's a cute idea. Like mine about the cuffs—

in your imagination you can always go home with the prettiest girl at the party, but at the party sometimes that is not true.

Now let's go on to the third beat. What's the third beat? How do we answer that question?

STUDENT:     Go back to the main objective, *to win the respect of the instructor*.

MAMET:       Absolutely. Now: let's approach this differently. What's a *bad* idea for the third beat?

STUDENT:     *Waiting*.

MAMET:       *Waiting* is a bad idea for the third beat.

STUDENT:     *Preparing* is a bad idea for the third beat.

MAMET:       Yes, because we already did it. It's like climbing the stairs. We don't want to climb a stair we've already climbed. So *preparing again* is a bad idea. Why play the same beat twice? Get on with it. Everybody always says the way to make any movie better is burn the first reel, and it's true. All of us have this experience almost every time we go to the movies. Twenty minutes in, we say, "*why,* they should have started the movie *here*." Get on with it, for the love of Mike. Get into the scene late, get out of the scene early, tell the story in the cut. It's important to remember that it is not the dramatist's task to create confrontation or chaos but, rather, to create order. *Start* with the disordering event, and let the beat be about the attempt to restore order.

We're given the situation: this fellow wants such and so—he has an objective. That's enough chaos for you right there. He has an objective. He wants *to win the respect of his teacher*. This fellow *lacks* something. He's going to go out and get it.

Entropy is a logical progression toward the simplest, the most ordered state. So is drama.* The entropy, the drama, continues until a disordered state has been brought to rest. Things have been disordered, and they must come back to rest.

The disorder is not vehement in this case, it's fairly simple: someone wants a guy's respect. We don't have to worry about creating a problem. We make a better movie if we worry about restoring order. Because if we worry about creating problems, our protagonist's going to do things that are interesting. We don't want him to do that. We want him to do things that are logical.

What's the next step? What's the next beat going to be about? We're talking in terms of our particular progression. The first beat being *to arrive early*. The second one being *preparation,* to prepare. And the third one being? (Always thinking in terms of the superobjective of the movie, which is *to gain the respect of.* That's your test. That's the litmus test: *to gain the respect of.*)

STUDENT: To introduce himself?

---

*I know the dictionary defines entropy as a progression toward the most disordered state—but on this point, I take issue with that most excellent book.

MAMET: Mayhap the beat is about *greeting*. Yes, what do we call that kind of greeting?

STUDENT: Acknowledgment . . . ?

STUDENT: Ingratiation . . . ?

MAMET: To ingratiate, to pay homage to, to acknowledge, to greet, to make contact. Which, of all these, is most specific to the superobjective *to gain the respect of*?

STUDENT: I think *homage*.

MAMET: All right, then. Let's make up a little photo essay about *homage* here. The deeper you can think, the better it's going to be. Deeper in the sense of writing means "what would it be like to me?" Not "how might anyone pay homage?" but "what does the idea of homage mean to *me*?" That's what makes art different from decoration.

What would be real homage?

STUDENT: The professor arrives, and our guy goes to shake his hand.

MAMET: Okay. But this is like the watch, isn't it? Earliness— *watch*. Homage—*handshake*. There's nothing wrong with it, but let's think a little bit deeper, because we might as well, now that we have the luxury of time.

What would be a lovely way to show homage, a way that really *means* something to you? Because if you want it to mean something to the audience, it should mean something to you. They are like you— they are human beings: if it don't mean something to *you,* it ain't going to mean something to *them.* The movie is a dream. The movie should be *like* a dream. So if we start thinking in terms of dreams instead of in terms of television, what might we say? We're going to have a little photo essay, a little documentary about *homage.*

STUDENT: When you say a dream, you mean it doesn't have to be believable in the sense that someone would actually do it in real life?

MAMET: No, I mean . . . I don't know how far we can stretch this theory, but let's find out, let's stretch it till it breaks. At the end of *Places in the Heart,* Robert Benton put a sequence that is one of the strongest things in an American movie in a long time. It's the sequence where we see everyone who was killed in the film is now alive again. He's created something that is like a dream in this. He is juxtaposing scenes that are discontinuous, and that juxtaposition gives us a third idea. The first scene being *everyone's dead.* The second scene being *everyone's alive.* The juxtaposition creates the idea of *a great wish,* and the audience says, "oh my God, why can't things be that way?" That's like a dream. Like when Cocteau has the hands coming out of the wall. It's better than following the protagonist around, isn't it?

In *House of Games,* when the two guys are fighting about a gun in the doorway and we cut away to a shot of the sidekick, the professor character, looking on, *then* you hear the gunshot. That's pretty good filmmaking. It wasn't great filmmaking, maybe, but it was a lot better than television. Right? It gives us the idea. They're fighting; you cut to the guy looking. The idea is *what's going to happen* and *we can't do anything about it.*

It conveys the idea of *helplessness,* which is what the beat is about. The protagonist is helpless: we get it without following her around. We put the *protagonist* in the same position as the *audience*— through the *cut*—by making the viewer create the idea himself, in his own mind, as Eisenstein told us.

STUDENT: How about if the student presents something to the professor? Some kind of special present. Or he bows when the guy comes in, and offers him a chair?

MAMET: No, you're trying to tell it in the *shot.* We want to tell it in the cut. How about this—the first shot is at the level of feet, a tracking shot of a pair of feet walking. And the second shot is a close-up of the protagonist, seated, and he turns his head quickly. What does the juxtaposition of the two things give us?

STUDENT: Arrival.

MAMET: And?

STUDENT: Recognition.

MAMET: Yeah; it's not quite *homage,* it's attentiveness or *attention.* At least, it's two shots creating a third idea. The first shot has to contain the idea of where the feet are. The feet are a little bit distant, right? With the idea that the feet are distant and the fellow hears them anyway, what does the juxtaposition of these two things give us?

STUDENT:    Awareness.

MAMET:    *Awareness;* perhaps not *homage,* but *awareness* or great attention, which might just sneak up on *homage.* What about if we had the long shot of the feet coming down the corridor and then a shot of our guy standing up? It shows a little bit more homage, in that he's standing up.

STUDENT:    Especially if he were to stand up in a humble way.

MAMET:    He doesn't have to do it in a humble way. All we have to show is him standing up. He doesn't have to stand up any way at all; all he has to do is stand up. The juxtaposition of that and the shot of the other guy far off gives the idea of homage.

STUDENT:    How about when the guy stands up he bows his head?

MAMET:    It doesn't really tell any more. And it's more inflected, which is to say worse for the purpose of filmmaking. The more we "inflect" or "load" the shot, the less powerful the cut is going to be. Anyone else?

STUDENT:    A shot over the protagonist with a notebook. He looks up, stands up, and runs out of the shot. A shot of our hallway and the door in the hallway, which has a glass window to it. Protagonist runs into the shot and opens the door just as a man walks in the other direction.

MAMET:    Yes. Good. I see you like that. Two questions we

might ask ourselves—one question is *does that convey the idea of homage?* and the other is *do I like it?* If you ask the second question, you say, well, heck, I don't know if I like it or not. Am I a fellow with good taste? Yes. Does this have as much good taste in it as I think I have in myself? Gosh, I don't know. I'm lost.

The question you *do* want to ask is *does it convey the idea of homage?* If it does convey the idea of homage, then go on to the next step: *do I like it?* There is the inner ability Stanislavsky called the "judge of yourself," which one might characterize as a certain amount of artistic good taste. That's going to function anyway because we all have good taste. It's the nature of the human being to please. We all want to please one another. Nobody doesn't want that. There's no one who doesn't want to succeed. What we're trying to do is make our subconscious work for us by making that task at which we can succeed very simple and very technical so we don't have to throw ourselves on the mercy of either our good taste or the cinema-going public.

We want to have some test that allows us to know when our job is done without relying on our good taste. That test here is *does it convey the idea of homage?* Feet way off, man stands up. I think it does. Let's go on to the next beat. What's the next beat after *homage?* What's the first question we want to ask?

STUDENT:   What's the superobjective?

MAMET:     Good. What's the answer?

STUDENT:   *To win the respect of the professor.*

MAMET:     So after showing homage, what's the next beat?

STUDENT:   *To impress.*

MAMET:     It's a tad general. It also rather reiterates the superobjective. *To impress, to win respect.* They are too similar. One part at a time. The boat has to look like a boat; the sail doesn't have to look like a boat. Make each part do its job, and the original purpose of the totality will be achieved—as if by magic. Make the beats serve the scene, and the scene will be done; make the scenes, in the same way, the building blocks of the film, and the film will be done. Don't make the beat do the service of the whole, don't try to reiterate the play in the scene. It's like "would anyone like a cup of coffee because I'm Irish," right? It's how most acting is done today. "I'm so glad to see you today because, as you'll find out later, I'm a mass murderer." Anyone? The next beat?

STUDENT:   *To gain acknowledgment?*

MAMET:     That's also rather general.

STUDENT:   *To please?*

MAMET:     You can't get more general than that.

STUDENT:   *To show affection?*

MAMET:     *To gain respect by showing affection?* Maybe; what else?

STUDENT:   *To show self-confidence?*

MAMET:     Be dynamic. See, these things you suggest really

could come at more or less any point, and they will betray us into a circularity more appropriate to the epic than to the dramatic form. But what will be the *next essential thing* to come after *showing homage?*

STUDENT:   *To blow your own horn?*

MAMET:   Would you do that to gain someone's respect?

STUDENT:   No.

MAMET:   You can ask yourself the question thusly: what would *I* like to do in the best of all possible worlds to earn someone's respect? It's a question of what you might do in your wildest imagination, not what you might do because you are bound by the strictures of polite behavior. We don't want our movies to be bound by that. We'd like our movies to be greatly expressive of our fantasy life.

There's another question we probably need to ask at this point. We might ask ourselves *when are we going to be done?* so we will know when the movie is done. We could go on trying *to gain respect* indefinitely. So we need a cap. Without a cap, the essential problem of the throughline, which is *to gain respect*, really can lead into a never-ending spiral, which is capped only by our good taste. So perhaps we need a throughline with a more positive, that is to say a more *definite* end than *to gain respect*.

For example, *getting a reward. Reward* being a simple and physically identifiable sign of respect. On this level of abstraction, the reward could be, for example, what?

STUDENT: It could be that he wants the teacher to do him a favor.

MAMET: Okay; anybody else?

STUDENT: He wants the teacher to give him a job.

MAMET: Yes; anything else?

STUDENT: The teacher gives him a pat on the back.

MAMET: That's not as specific as the first two, is it? I take it .that you're speaking rhetorically. In which case *the pat on the back* is similar *to gain his respect* in this: it is deficient in that it lacks a *cap* or an objective, so that one is unsure when one is finished. It's going to make our task a lot easier if we always know both *where we're going* and *when we're finished.* If the *job* is the objective, then when that *job* is given or when that job is absolutely denied, the scene will be over.

Or perhaps we could say the *reward* the student requires is this: he wants the teacher to change a grade. Then, when the teacher changes the grade, the scene will be over; or if the teacher categorically refuses to change the grade and no hope is left, then the scene would be over. So we could say that the throughline of the scene in that case is *to get a retraction.* Then *that's* what everything in the scene would be about.

What's the first thing that's done *to get a retraction?* *To show up early,* right? What's the second thing? *To prepare.* The third beat is *to pay homage.* It's going to be a lot easier to find out what the fourth beat is for *to get a retraction* than *to gain his respect,* because now we have a specific test for *knowing* when the movie will be over; we know where we have to end up, and we can find a beat that will lead us to that end. Does anybody know what a MacGuffin is?

STUDENT:   It's Hitchcock's phrase for a little invented device that will carry the action.

MAMET:   Yes. In a melodrama—Hitchcock's movies are melodramatic thrillers—a MacGuffin is *that thing which the hero is chasing.* The secret documents . . . the great seal of the republic of blah-blah-blah . . . the delivery of the secret message . . . We, the audience, never really know what it is. You are never told more specifically than "it's the secret documents."

Why should you be? We'll fill in for ourselves, unconsciously, those secret documents which are important to us.

In *The Uses of Enchantment,* Bruno Bettelheim says of fairy tales the same thing Alfred Hitchcock said about thrillers: that the *less* the hero of the play is inflected, identified, and characterized, the more we will endow him with our own internal meaning— the more we will *identify* with him—which is to say the more we will be assured that *we* are that hero.

"The hero rode up on a white horse." You don't say "a short hero rode up on a white horse," because if the listener isn't short he isn't going to identify with that hero. You don't say "a tall hero rode up on a white horse," because if the listener isn't tall, he won't identify with the hero. You say "a hero," and the audience subconsciously realize *they are* that hero.

The MacGuffin is *that thing which is important to us*—that most essential thing. The audience will supply it, each member for himself.

Just so in the objective *to get a retraction*. It's perhaps not necessary to know at this point a retraction of what.

The actor doesn't have to know it. A retraction of a grade, a retraction of a statement, a retraction of a reprimand. It's a MacGuffin at this point. The less the objective is inflected, the better off we, the audience, are. The less the hero is described to us, the better off we are.

Step four, anybody? We know where we're going, and we know who's going with us. We know who we love, but the devil knows who we'll marry. *To get a retraction.* Tally-ho, then, me hearties.

STUDENT: You have *to ask for the retraction.*

MAMET: Good. Now, wasn't that a breath of fresh air? The invigorating infusion of fresh air that this direct and blunt beat brings into this discussion is the same breath of fresh air that it will bring into the film. Now we have: *to show up early, to prepare, to pay homage,* and *to ask for* as the four beats of the story *to get a retraction.*

STUDENT:    Don't you think showing up early and preparing are the same as paying homage?

MAMET:    You are saying that these may be subsumed under the larger beat *to pay homage?* I don't know. I have a question about *to prepare,* which we may come back to. Now you see that the process we're going through here is re-forming the large to better understand the small, and re-forming the small to better understand the large (working from the superobjective to the beats, and reworking from the beats to the superobjective, et cetera), until we come up with a design that seems to fulfill all of our requirements. Then we'll put that design into action and we will shoot it.*

Now, we may find, as I found a little bit in my first movie and to a greater extent in my second, that after we've shot it we have to refine it further—which phenomenon scientists call the Jesus Factor,

---

*The process we are going through in this room is the exploration of the dynamic between the *moment* and the *objective.* It is this dynamic that, in this discussion, in film, in the theater, gives both the moment and the entirety strength—in the beautiful drama, each moment serves the purpose of the superobjective, and each moment is beautiful in itself. If the moment only serves the superobjective, we have plodding narrative pseudodrama, good only for object-lesson or "message" plays. If the moment only stands for itself, we have only self-indulgent or "performance" art. The effort that the dramatic artist spends in *analysis* frees both him and the audience to enjoy the play. If this time is not spent, the theater becomes the most dreadful of marriage beds, in which one party whimpers "love me," and the other pouts "convince me."

a technical term meaning "it works correctly on paper but for some reason doesn't work when we get it on its feet."

That happens sometimes. All you can do then is try to learn from it. The answer is always there. Sometimes it requires more wisdom than we possess at that instant—but the answer is always there. Sometimes the answer is: "I'm not smart enough to figure it out yet," and we must remember that the man said, "A poem is never finished—only abandoned."

All right, enough lovemaking. We got our three beats and looked at the throughline and said, "perhaps this throughline is not very good." We re-formed the throughline away from *to gain respect* and decided that it was *to get a retraction*. Now we can look back at the beats, and we may say that perhaps *preparing* is out of order. Perhaps *paying homage* is what that beat is about. I don't know. Let's forge on a little bit and see if the fourth step gives us some more clues.

STUDENT: Do we have to decide what the end result is?

MAMET: You mean does the hero get the retraction? Who's interested to know if he gets the retraction or not? Anyone?

STUDENT: I'd want to know, because then we can do something with the response of the teacher to the homage. Does the teacher know why the guy's there? Is he suspicious of—

MAMET:     No, no, no, forget the teacher; let's stick with the
           protagonist. We stick with the protagonist, and that
           will tell us the story. Because the story is *his* story.
           We're here not to create disorder but to create
           order. What's the inherent disorder? "The other
           guy has something I want." What does the other
           guy have? The power to issue a retraction. When
           is the story *over*? When the hero *gets* it. The disorder
           is inherent in the story. What we're trying to do is
           create order. When the hero either gets a retraction
           or finds that he cannot have a retraction, order will
           be restored. The story will be over, and there will
           be no further reason to be interested. Up to that
           point, what we're trying to do is bring about that
           blessed state of bliss in which there is no story. For
           as Mr. Trollope told us, "they are most happy who
           have no story to tell."
               Let's go on. Let's be jolly, jolly scientists and take
           one step at a time. The next step we've suggested
           is *to ask for*. What are some alternatives?

STUDENT:   *To plead his case.*

MAMET:     *To plead his case.* Now, as you see, we're suggesting
           two stories of two different lengths. Why? *To plead
           his case* is eventually going to have to contain *to ask*,
           right? And this is what determines the length of the
           healthy story—it is determined by the least number
           of steps absolutely essential to secure the hero's
           objective. Who likes which beat better—*to ask for*

or *to plead his case?* On what basis can we determine which is better for the story?

STUDENT: On the basis of why he's asking for the retraction?

MAMET: No. We don't care why. It's a MacGuffin he's asking for. Because he needs it.

STUDENT: But we don't know anything about it.

MAMET: I don't think we need to. Anybody think we need to? What you're talking about is what the illiterate call the "back story." You don't need it. Remember that the model of the drama is the dirty joke. This joke begins: "A traveling salesman stops at a farmer's door"—it does *not* begin: "Who would think that the two most disparate occupations of agriculture and salesmanship would one day be indissolubly united in our oral literature? Agriculture, that most solitary of pursuits, engendering the qualities of self-reliance and reflection; and salesmanship, in which . . ." Does the protagonist have to explain why he wants a retraction? To whom is he going to explain it? To the audience? Does that help him *get* it? No. He must only do those things that help him *get* a retraction. All he has to do is *get a retraction.* The guy says to the girl, "That's a lovely dress"— he does not say, "I haven't been laid in six weeks." Now, the question is: on what basis can we decide which is better in this beat—to *plead his case* or *to ask?* My feeling is *to plead his case* is better. Why? Because I'm having a good time and I'd like the story to go on a little bit longer. I don't think I have any better basis than that, and I think that that's all right. But I'd better check, because I know that I have a capacity for self-delusion. So the question I ask myself is, "does it run afoul of any of the rules we've discussed to use *to plead his case* rather than *to ask* at this point?" I check my rules, and my answer is No, so I'll choose the one I like.

STUDENT: Since pleading is more inflected, isn't that an attempt to be more interesting?

MAMET: I don't think so; and I don't think it's either more or less inflected. I think it's just different. I think it's a choice. You could say *to plead his case;* you could say *to present his case.* By the way, we didn't say these beats had to be uninflected. We said that the *shots* had to be uninflected. *Paying homage* may or may not have certain inherent psychological overtones. We talked about *to plead, to ask, to plead his case, to present his case.* Each of these is going to call up associations in the actor. It is these personal, immediate associations, by the way, that both induce the actor to act and keep him in line with the intentions of the author. *This* is what brings the actor to the play—not those gyrations of emotional self-abuse that hack teachers have fobbed off as *preparation.*

STUDENT: How about *to bargain,* or *to bribe?*

MAMET: What about these ideas, in terms of the structure?

Let's talk about *to bargain,* because that's a little bit simpler.

STUDENT: The problem is that we started with a different throughline. *Bargaining* wouldn't work with *gaining respect,* but it might be a way to get a *retraction.*

MAMET: This is a problem you're going to run into a lot in dramatic structure. Because if you are creating it, either creating a film of your own or taking someone's film and trying to find the inherent dramatic structure in it, no angel is going to come down to you and say, "this is the throughline." What's going to happen is *exactly* this process of wondering and revising—to work every time either to create or to discern a throughline.

We've decided now that *to get a retraction* is the throughline of the scene. We are on to the beat following *to prepare.* Perhaps this next beat is *to present the case.* So this is now our new beat. What a relief to get on to this new beat. What self-respect we must feel for taking upon ourselves the onus of this task so as to save the audience the trouble. *To present the case.*

Our task now is to find a series of uninflected shots that will give us this idea: *to present the case.* The student wants to present the case to the teacher. Now, where are we going to find a clue? We have four beats. We're working on the fourth beat. What is going to be our clue to the answer of the shots?

Some helpful hint we might find to the answer of *presenting the case.*

STUDENT: How we *prepared?*

MAMET: Exactly so. The previous beat will provide a clue. It was *to prepare.* The beat that we thought, in terms of the new throughline, might possibly be dorky may, in effect, offer us quite a hint. So let's go back and look at our shot list for *to prepare.* It would be nice for the sake of cleanliness if we knew whether there was something we were wasting in there. Some *extra* step, which weakened *to prepare* but might strengthen *to present the case.* Like Indians of yore, we want to use all parts of the buffalo.

STUDENT: The shot where he opens the notebook, has the little strip with the cardboard things, rips them, writes on one, puts it in the tab holder.

MAMET: Good. Now, what are the shots for *to present the case?*

STUDENT: The presentation of the notebook in some way.

MAMET: What are the actual shots? A guy comes into a room, a guy in the room approaches the desk. Our criterion is that a juxtaposition of shots will give us the idea we require in this instance, *to present the case.* We have to know what we're taking a picture of.

STUDENT: Start with a shot of a desk with nothing on it and the notebook is pushed in.

MAMET: What's the next shot?

STUDENT: The reaction from the teacher. Either approval or disapproval.

MAMET:       No. All this beat has to be about is *presenting the case*. We don't need the teacher's reaction here.

STUDENT:     If the first shot were a presentation of the book and the second shot the teacher looking down, wouldn't the juxtaposition of those two shots present the case to him?

MAMET:       Maybe the first shot is the empty desk and a book is placed into it, and the second shot is the teacher at the desk looks down at the book and he also looks up, and we cut to a shot of the student. I think we need the student there because he *presents the case*.

STUDENT:     But couldn't we recognize the notebook from scene two? We know it's the same student we saw preparing, so we don't need a shot of him.

MAMET:       The book is identification enough?

STUDENT:     Yeah; we know it's the student's book. The book stands for the student.

MAMET:       Very good. Of course, you're right. I got caught up in the idea of following the protagonist around. Good. Now, this brings us to the application of the principle of the throughline to the plastic elements of production.

  What music is playing? What time of day or night is it? What do the costumes and the sets look like? At one point you mentioned someone reading a magazine. You say a magazine: *what* magazine? I'm not overstating the case; because somebody makes these decisions, and that person is called the director. The prop person is going to say, "what should the notebook look like?" and what are you, the director, going to say? First off, what is the untutored person going to say? "Golly, the scene is about *to get a retraction,* so what kind of notebook does a person who wants to get a retraction carry?" If this seems dorky, if this seems overstated to you, look at American movies. Because that's the way all American movies are made. "Hi, how are you today because I just got back from Vietnam." In Hollywood, a committee of thugs wants to make sure that each word, moment, shot, prop, sound, et cetera, in a movie will stand for and, in effect, advertise the film. This committee is called "producers," and they are to the arts what the ducking stool was to jurisprudence.*

What answer do we give to the prop person who says "what's the notebook look like?" What are you going to say?

---

*Natural, creative exuberance and self-confidence are wonderful things in an artist. They are inhibited from growing into arrogance not through the content but because of the process of education. Even the minimally serious artist is humbled constantly by the screaming demands of craft.

Those who style themselves "producers" have not had the benefit of any such education, and their arrogance knows no bounds. They are like the white slave owners of old, sitting on their porches with their cooling drinks and going on about the inherent laziness of the Negro race. The "producer," having never had a run-in with the demands of a craft, sees all ideas as basically equal and his own as first among them, for no reason other than that he has thought of it. This notion is easier to fathom if one thinks

STUDENT: Doesn't it depend on what the objective is or isn't?

MAMET: No, because you can't make a "retraction notebook" any more than you can act what room you just came out of—though there are, to their shame, schools of acting that purport to teach such. What should the notebook look like—this "retraction note-book"?

STUDENT: Put a label on the cover?

MAMET: The audience won't read it. It's like a sign. The audience doesn't want to read a sign; they want to watch a motion picture, in which the story is advanced through the cut.

STUDENT: They don't have to read it. It's a black folder, white label, looks like a book report.

MAMET: Why should it look like a book report? I mean, it's not a bad idea that it should look like a book report, but why is it a *good* idea that it look like a book report? Prop person says, "what does it look like?"

---

back to the period of early adolescence and to, perhaps, the critique of an English teacher who said of our efforts: "I don't understand" or "It is unclear," of which correction one thought: "The old fool . . . *I* know what I meant."

I have a great deal of pride and, I suppose, a large admixture of arrogant pride. I, in my generally losing contest with these self-styled "producers," many times console myself by thinking that after society falls apart, I will be able to eke out at least my meals and shelter by putting on plays that may make people laugh; but that these "producers" would have to wait until I and those like me went to work before they could eat.

Yes, that is how I see "producers." They are "let me take that cow to the fair for you, son."

What's the correct answer? What does it do? What does the *report* do?

STUDENT: It *presents the case.*

MAMET: Right. Now, what's the shot list for presenting the case?

STUDENT: The open book on the desk.

MAMET: What's the next shot?

STUDENT: The face of the teacher.

MAMET: What is not the next shot? The face of the student, right? So, therefore, how does the book look?

STUDENT: Prepared.

MAMET: No, you can't make the book look prepared. You can make it look *neat.* That might be nice, but that's not the most important thing for your answer to the prop person.* Think about the shot list and the objective *to present the case.* To make it prepared, to make it neat, to make it convincing, the audience ain't going to notice. What are they going to notice?

STUDENT: That it's the same book they've seen already.

MAMET: So what's your answer to the prop person?

STUDENT: Make it recognizable.

MAMET: Exactly so! Good! *You've got to be able to recognize it.* That is the most important thing about this report. This is how you use the principle of throughline to

---

*The audience will accept anything they have not been given a reason to disbelieve. So the report must look, minimally, neat, for if it did not, the audience might question the sincerity of the hero's desire. The neatness of the report is an *antiseptic* rather than a *creative* consideration.

answer questions about the set and to answer questions about the costumes. The book *in general* is not important. What's important is what it does in the scene. The most blatant thing it does in the scene is *present the case*. Since we aren't going to see a shot of the student, it's got to *present the case* for him. That shot of the uninflected book has to present the case. Since we know that it has to be uninflected, the answer cannot be "it's a *prepared* book." The answer cannot be "it's a contrite book." The answer must be "it's got to be the same book we saw in shot two." In choosing the book, you are telling the audience *that thing without which they cannot understand the movie.* In this case, it's the essential element of the shot. *That without which the beat will not survive* is that it's the same notebook as in the previous beat. It is essential to the telling of the story.

Every time you make a choice as a director, it must be based on whether the thing in question is essential to telling the story. If we don't need the shot of the student, then we'd better be jolly, jolly sure that they understand that it's the same book.

The audience is only going to look at the most overriding thing in the frame. You must take charge of and direct their attention. It's also the principle of magic: What is the single important thing? Make it easy for them to see it, and you're doing your job. You don't have to make it a book about *getting your retraction*. You do have to make it the same notebook. So our beats are *to show up early, to prepare, to pay homage, to present the case.* What were the shots for *to show up early?*

STUDENT:   He arrives and tries the doorknob.

MAMET:   No. I hope you don't think I'm being picayune, but it's very useful to think of the film in exactly the same way the audience is going to perceive the film. What they're going to see in the first shot is *a man walking down the hall.* What are the shots?

STUDENT:   Man walks down hall, shot of a hand on a doorknob, same man sits down on a bench.

MAMET:   Perfect. Now, why did all those Olympic skaters fall down? The only answer I know is that they hadn't practiced enough. Practice with these tools until you find them boring, then practice some more. Here is a tool—choose your shots, beats, scenes, objectives, and *always* refer to them by the names you chose.

What are the shots for *to prepare?*

STUDENT:   Man takes the notebook out, rips out a tab, writes something down on a tab, puts the tab in the plastic thing, closes the tab.

MAMET:   Good. *To pay homage?*

STUDENT:   Shot of the man looking and getting up out of the frame. A shot of the man running to a glass door. He opens the door, a man walks through.

MAMET:   Good. Next beat?

STUDENT:   *To present the case.* An empty desk. The notebook put on the desk, and a shot of the man sitting at the desk, looking down at it.

MAMET: Good. Let's finish it now. How do we reach a conclusion?

STUDENT: The teacher could start considering the book.

MAMET: What is the beat we are trying to dramatize here?

STUDENT: *Judgment.*

MAMET: Okay, the idea is *judgment. Consideration* is a different way of saying it. But the teacher considering the book doesn't really have any weight of montage behind it. It's basically expository. A guy picks up evidence and looks at it and makes up his own mind. Not good storytelling, as Aristotle told us. The character shouldn't "just get the idea."

STUDENT: Why is the next beat *judgment,* if all the way through, the beats are about the student and the teacher? Don't you want to follow the course of the student and not the teacher?

MAMET: What's your idea?

STUDENT: I saw the beat as *taking a stand.* He's presented the case, and you cut to him standing there, and he's not going to take no for an answer. And you cut back to the teacher looking up at the kid.

MAMET: What are some other ideas for the next beat?

STUDENT: *Receipt of the retraction.*

MAMET: Yeah, that's an idea.

STUDENT: *To be denied.*

MAMET: That's not really the beat; that's the result. That's

the end of some other beat. The student/protagonist
has to be working toward completion.

STUDENT: At this point in the story, you are going to expect
the response of the professor. The next logical beat
after *presenting the case* is judgment, *judging the case.*
When that beat is over, he has or hasn't gotten the
retraction. We don't have to follow the student to
complete the throughline, do we?

MAMET: No.

STUDENT: But it's the kid's job to get a retraction.

MAMET: Yes, it is. But it doesn't have to be a picture of the
kid. We want to know what happens next in terms
of the throughline, not in terms of what the protagonist does. What was our last shot in the last
beat?

STUDENT: The professor looking down at the book.

MAMET: The professor's looking down. Cut to a shot of a
bunch of kids in the doorway. A new kid comes,
and they all look over to one side or another. We
cut to their point of view of the empty classroom
with the kid sitting there and the professor looking
at him. To get to the idea of judgment. Now we're
ready for the resolution. We see the professor in a
long shot, he opens the book, he looks down to his
right, we cut to the desk drawer, we see him open
the desk drawer and he takes out a stamp pad. You
see him stamp the book. And you cut to a shot of
the kid, who is smiling, and he picks up the book,
and we cut to a shot of the kid's hand closing the

book, and then from the back of the classroom you see the kid go to his seat and the professor stand and call the rest of the class, and they go in, and they sit down. All right?

STUDENT: What if he *didn't get the retraction?*

MAMET: I don't know. It's our first movie. Let's make it a happy ending, what the hell. And now we're done, and that was excellent work.

# 3

# COUNTERCULTURAL

# ARCHITECTURE AND DRAMATIC

# STRUCTURE

I was a student in the turbulent sixties in Vermont at a countercultural college. In that time and place, there flourished something called a school of Countercultural Architecture. Some people back then thought that traditional architecture had been too stifling, and so they designed and built a lot of counterculture buildings. These buildings proved unlivable. Their design didn't begin with the idea of the building's purpose; it began with the idea of how the architect "felt."

As those architects looked at their countercultural buildings over the years, they may have reflected that there's a reason for traditional design. There's a reason that doors are placed in a certain way, there's a reason that sills are made a certain way. All those countercultural buildings may have expressed the intention of the architect, but they didn't serve the purpose of the inhabitants. They all either fell down or are falling down or should be torn down. They're a blot on the landscape and they don't age gracefully and every passing year underscores the jejune folly of those countercultural architects.

I live in a house that is two hundred years old. It was built with an axe, by hand, and without nails. Barring some sort of man-made catastrophe, it will be standing in another two hundred years. It was built with an understanding of, and a respect for, wood, weather, and human domestic requirements.

It's very difficult to shore up something that has been done badly. You'd better do your planning up front, when you have the time. It's like working with glue. When it sets, you've used up your time. When it's almost set, you then have to make quick decisions under pressure. If you design a chair correctly, you can put all the time into designing it correctly and assemble it at your leisure. In fact, the ancient chairmakers—which is to say chairmakers up until about the turn of the century— used to make their chairs without glue because they correctly understood not only the nature of joints but the nature of woods. They knew which woods would shrink and which would expand with age, so that these woods, when correctly combined, would make the chair stronger over time.

I recognized two things in finishing up my second movie. When you're doing the movie, after you finish with the shot list but before you start shooting it, you have a period called "preproduction." In preproduction, you say, "you know what would be a good idea? To really make the audience understand that we're in a garage, what about a sign that says 'garage.'"

So you meet with your art department and you talk a lot about signs and you make up a lot of signs. I made two movies and I made up a lot of signs. You never see the signs in a movie—never. You just never see them. They are after-the-fact attempts to shore up that which was not correctly designed. Another handy but useless "reminder" tool is the process of looping, or ADR (Automatic Dialogue Reading—dialogue recorded and inserted after the movie has been shot), to communicate to the audience information the film lacks. For example, dubbing words into somebody's mouth when we see his back on the screen. To wit: "oh, look, here we go down that staircase that we're trying to get to the bottom of." That never works either. Why? Because all that the audience cares about is *what is the thrust of the scene*—what does the hero want? More precisely, what is the essential aspect of the shot? They aren't there to look at signs, and they won't look at them. You can't force them to look at them. It is the nature of human perception to go to the most interesting thing; and just as we know in terms of the dirty joke, the most interesting thing is *what happens next* in the story that you promised the audience you were going to tell them. You can't make them stop and look at that sign. They don't care to indulge you by listening to your looping, so you'd better do your work beforehand.

That work is done in understanding the nature of the materials and using that understanding in the design of the film. That's basically what a film is; it's a design. You know, all these personally felt statements of people who try to put a lot of garbage into the shot and pan around a bunch to show how moved they are by their chosen subject: these are just like countercultural architecture. They may be a personal statement, but they don't serve the turn of the inhabitants or, in this case, the turn of the viewers who would like to know *what happens next.* You tax the audience every time you don't move on to the next essential step of the progression as quickly as possible. You're taxing their good nature. They may indulge you for political reasons—which is what most of modern art is about. Political reasons being, "dammit, I *like* those kinds of bad movies" or "I *like* that kind of countercultural statement. I am one of that group, and I endorse the other members of this group, who appreciate the sort of things this fellow is trying to say." The audience can endorse the triviality of modern art, but they can't like it. I suggest you think about the difference between the way people talk about any performance artist and the way they talk about Cary Grant. And to you lovely enthusiasts who will aver that the purpose of modern art is not to be liked, I respond, "oh, grow up."

The job of the film director is *to tell the story through the juxtaposition of uninflected images*—because that is the essential nature of the medium. It operates best through that juxtaposition, because that's the nature of human perception: to perceive two events, determine a progression, and want to know what happens next.

"Performance art" works, as it's the nature of human perception to order random images in favor of an overriding preconception. Another example of this is neurosis. Neurosis is the ordering of unrelated events or ideas or images in favor of an overriding preconception.

"I am," for example, "an unsightly person": that's the overriding preconception. Then, given any two unrelated events I can order them to make them mean *that*. "Oh, yes, I understand. This woman came out of the hall and did not seem to notice me and rushed into the elevator and quickly pushed the button and the elevator closed because I am an unattractive person." That's what neurosis is. It is the attempt of a disordered mind to apply the principle of cause and effect. This same attempt takes place subconsciously in the viewer of a drama.

If the lights go out and the curtain goes up, the overriding idea is "a play is taking place"; "someone is telling me a story."

The human brain, understanding that, will take all of the events in the play and form them into a story just as it forms perception into neurosis. It is the nature of human perception to connect unrelated images into a story, because we need to make the world make sense.

If the overriding idea is that *a play is taking place,* then we will form the images that we see between the time the curtain goes up and the time the curtain comes down *into* a play whether or not they have been structured as one. Just so with the movie, which is why bad filmmaking can "succeed." It is our nature to want to make sense of these events—we can't help it. The human mind would make sense of them even if they were a random juxtaposition.

This being the nature of human perception, the smart dramatist will use it to his or her advantage and say, "well, if the human mind is going to do all that anyway, why don't *I* do it first? Then I will be going with the flow rather than battling against the tide."

If you aren't telling a story, moving from one image to

another, the images have to be more and more "interesting" per se. If you *are* telling a story, then the human mind, as it's working along with you, is perceiving your thrust, both consciously and, more important, subconsciously. The audience members are going to go along with that story and will require neither inducement, in the form of visual extravagance, nor explanation, in the form of narration.

*They want to see what's happening next.* Is the guy going to get killed? Is the girl going to kiss him? Will they find the money buried in the old mine?

When the film is correctly designed, the subconscious and the conscious are in alignment, and we *need* to hear what happens next. The audience is ordering the events just as the author did, so we are in touch with both his conscious and his unconscious mind. We have become involved in the story.

If we don't care what happens next, if the film is *not* correctly designed, we may, unconsciously, create our own story in the same way that a neurotic creates his own cause-and-effect rendition of the world around him, but we're no longer interested in the story that we're being told. "Yes, I saw that the girl put the kettle on the fire and then a cat ran out on stage," we might say of "performance art." "Yes, I saw, but I don't quite know where it's going. I'm following it, but I am certainly not going to risk my unconscious well-being by becoming involved."

That's when it stops being interesting. So that's where the bad author, like the countercultural architect, has to take up the slack by making each subsequent event *more* diverting than the last; to trick the audience into paying attention.

The end of this is obscenity. Let's really see their genitals, let's really endanger the actor through stunts, let's really set the building on fire. Over the course of a movie, it forces the filmmaker to get more and more bizarre. Over the course of a career, it forces a filmmaker to get more and more outré; over the course of a culture, it forces the culture to degenerate into depravity, which is what we have now.

Interest in a film comes from this: the desire to find out what happens next. The less reality conforms to the neurotic's view, the more bizarre his explanation must become, the end of which development is psychosis—"performance art" or "modern theater" or "modern filmmaking."

The structure of any dramatic form should be a syllogism— which is a logical construct of this form: If A, then B. A play or movie proceeds from a statement: *"if A"* (in which a condition of unrest is created or posited), to a conclusion: *"then B"* (at which time entropy will once again rear its corrective head, and a condition of rest will have been once again achieved).

For example, as we've seen, if a student *needs a retraction,* he will pursue a series of actions that will lead him to the retraction or to an irrevocable denial of the retraction. And then he will be at rest; a condition of entropy will have been achieved.

This *entropy* is one of the most interesting aspects of our life as a whole. We are born, certain things happen, and we die. The sexual act is a perfectly good example. Things are called into motion that did not heretofore exist and that demand some form of resolution. Something is called into existence that did not heretofore exist, and then the unrest that this new thing creates has to be resolved, and when it's resolved, the life, the sexual act, the play, is done. That's how you know when it's time to go home.

The guy solved his problem at the whorehouse. The guy lost all his money at the racetrack. The couple was reunited. The bad king died. How do we know this is the end of the story? Because *the rise to power of the bad king* was the problem that we came to see solved. How do we know that *when they kiss* it's the end of the movie? Because it's a movie about the boy not getting the girl. The solution of the problem posited at the beginning of the experience is the end of the story. That's also how we know the scene is over, isn't it?

We said that the scene is the correct unit of study. If you understand the scene, you understand the play or movie. When the problem posited by the scene is over, the scene is over. A lot of times in movies you want to get out of the scene *before* the problem is over and have it answered in the *next* scene, as a matter of fact. Why? So that the audience will follow you. They, you will remember, want to know what happens next.

To get into the scene late and to get out early is to demonstrate respect for your audience. It's very easy to manipulate an audience—to be "better" than the audience—because you've got all the cards. "I don't have to tell you *anything;* I can change the story in midstream! I can be whatever I want. Go to hell!" But listen to the difference between the way people talk about films by Werner Herzog and the way they talk about films by Frank Capra, for example. One of them may or may not understand something or other, but the other understands what it is to tell a story, and he *wants* to tell a story, which is the nature of the dramatic art—to tell a story. That's all it's good for. People have tried for centuries to use drama to change people's lives, to influence, to comment, to express themselves. It doesn't work. It might be nice if it worked for those things, but it doesn't. The only thing the dramatic form is good for is telling a story.

If you want to tell a story, it might be a good idea to understand a little bit about the nature of human perception. Just as, if you want to know how to build a roof, it might be a good idea to understand a little bit about the effects of gravity and the effects of precipitation.

If you go up into Vermont and you build a roof with a peak, the snow will fall off. You build a flat roof, the roof will fall down from the weight of the snow—which is what happened to a lot of the countercultural architecture of the 1960s. "There may be a reason people have wanted to hear stories for ten million years," the performance artist says, "but I really don't *care,* because *I have something to say.*"

The film business is caught in a spiral of degeneracy because it's run by people who have no compass. And the only thing *you* can do in the face of this downward force is tell the truth. Anytime anyone tells the truth, that's a counterforce.

You cannot hide your objective. No one can hide. Contemporary American films are almost universally sloppy, trivial, and obscene. If your objective is to succeed in the "industry," your work, and your soul, will be exposed to these destructive influences. If you desperately crave acceptance by that industry, you will likely become those things.

The actor cannot hide his or her objective, neither can the

playwright, neither can the film director. If a person's objective is truly—and you don't have to do it humbly, because you'll get humble soon enough—*to understand the nature of the medium,* that objective will be communicated to the audience. How? Magically. I don't know how. Because it will. It just can't be hidden. In addition to what you will or will not learn about the medium through your desire to understand it, that desire *itself* will be manifested.

I carve wood sometimes. It's magical how the wooden object creates itself. One becomes enthralled by and very observant of the grain of the wood, and the piece tells you how to carve it.

Sometimes the piece is fighting back against you. If you're honest in making a movie, you'll find that it's often fighting back against you too. It's telling you how to write it. Just as we found in the "got a retraction" movie.

It's very, very difficult to do these very, very simple problems. They're fighting back against you, these problems, but the mastery of them is the beginning of the mastery of the art of film.

# 4

# THE TASKS OF THE

# DIRECTOR

## WHAT TO TELL THE
## ACTORS AND WHERE TO
## PUT THE CAMERA

I've seen directors do as many as sixty takes of a shot. Now, any director who's watched dailies knows that after the third or fourth take he can't remember the first; and on the set, when shooting the tenth take, you can't remember the purpose of the scene. And after shooting the twelfth, you can't remember why you were born. Why do directors, then, shoot this many takes? Because they don't know what they want to take a picture of. And they're frightened. If you don't know what you want, how do you know when you're done? If you know what you want, shoot it and sit down. Suppose you are directing the "get a retraction" movie. What are you going to tell the actor who does that first beat for you? What do we refer to; what is our compass here? What is a simple tool to which we may refer to answer this question?

To give direction to the actor, you do the same thing you do when you give direction to the cameraman. You refer to *the objective of the scene,* which in this case is *to get a retraction;* and to the meaning of this beat, which here is *to arrive early.*

Based on this, you tell the actor to do those things, and only those things, he needs to do for you to shoot the beat, *to arrive early.* You tell him to go to the door, try the door, and sit down. That is literally what you tell him. Nothing more.

Just as the shot doesn't have to be inflected, the acting doesn't have to be inflected, nor should it be. The acting should be a performance of the simple physical action. Period. Go to the door, try the door, sit down. He doesn't have to walk down the hall respectfully. This is the greatest lesson anyone can ever teach you about acting. Perform the physical motions called for by the script as simply as possible. Do *not* "help the play along."

He doesn't have to sit down respectfully. He doesn't have to turn the door respectfully. The script is doing that work. The more the actor tries to make each physical action carry the meaning of the "scene" or the "play," the more that actor is ruining your movie. The nail doesn't have to look like a house; it is not a house. It is a *nail.* If the house is going to stand, the nail must do the work of a nail. To do the work of the nail, it has to *look* like a nail.

The more the actor is giving him or herself over to the specific uninflected physical action, the better off your movie is, which is why we like those old-time movie stars so much. They were awfully damn simple. "What do I do in this scene?"

was their question. Walk down the hall. How? Fairly quickly. Fairly slowly. Determinedly. Listen to those simple adverbs— the choice of actions and adverbs constitutes the craft of directing actors.

What's the scene? *To get a retraction.* What's the meaning of the beat? *To arrive early.* What are the specific shots? Guy walking down the hall, guy tries the doorknob, guy sits down. Good luck will be the residue of good design. When the actor says, "how do I walk down the hall?" you say, "I don't know . . . quickly." Why do you say that? Because your subconscious is working on the problem. Because you've paid your dues at this point and you're entitled to make what may seem to be an arbitrary decision but may also be a subconscious solution to a problem; and you have honored the subconscious by referring the problem to it long enough for it to cough up the answer.

Just as it's in the nature of the audience to want to help the story along, to help along good work, that is to say work which is respectful of its inner nature, just so it's in the nature of your subconscious to want to help this task along. A lot of decisions that you think are going to be made arbitrarily are arrived at through the simple and dedicated workings of your subconscious. When you look back at them, you will say, "well, I got lucky there, didn't I?" and the answer will be "yes" because you paid for it. You paid for that subconscious help when you agonized over the structure of the film. The shot list.

Actors will ask you a lot of questions. "What am I thinking here?" "What's my motivation?" "Where did I just come from?" The answer to all of these questions is *it doesn't matter.* It doesn't matter because you can't act on those things. I defy anyone to act where he just came from. If you can't act on it, why think about it? Instead, your best bet is to ask the actor to do his simple physical actions as simply as possible.

"Please walk down the hall, try the doorknob." You don't have to say "try the doorknob and it's locked." Just try the doorknob and sit down. Movies are made out of very simple ideas. The good actor will perform each small piece as completely and as simply as possible.

Most actors are, unfortunately, not good actors. There are many reasons for this, the prime reason being that theater has fallen apart in our lifetime. When I was young, most actors, by the time they got to be thirty, had spent ten years on the stage, earning their living.

Actors don't do that anymore, so they never get a chance to learn how to act well. Virtually all of our actors in this country are badly trained. They're trained to take responsibility for the scene, to be emotional, to use each role to audition for the next. To make each small and precious moment on the stage or screen both "mean" the whole play and display their wares, to act, in effect, "sit down because I'm the king of France." It's not that actors are dumb people. To the contrary, the job, in my experience, attracts folk of high intelligence, and most of them are dedicated people; bad actors and good actors are in the main dedicated and hardworking people. Unfortunately, most actors don't accomplish much, because they're badly trained, underemployed, and anxious both to advance their career and to "do good."

Also, most actors try to use their intellectuality to portray the idea of the movie. Well, that's not their job. Their job is to accomplish, *beat by beat,* as simply as possible, the specific action set out for them by the script and the director.

The purpose of rehearsal is to tell the actors *exactly* the actions called for, beat by beat.

When you get on the set, the good actors who took careful notes will show up, *do* those actions—not *emote,* not *discover,* but do what they're getting paid to do, which is to perform, as simply as possible, exactly the thing they rehearsed.

If you, the director, understand the theory of montage, you don't have to strive to bring the actors to a real or pretended state of frenzy or love or hate or anything emotional. It's not the actor's job to be emotional—it is the actor's job to be *direct.*

Acting and dialogue fall into the same boat. Just as with the acting, the purpose of the dialogue is not to pick up the slack in the shot list. The purpose of dialogue is not to carry information about the "character." The only reason people speak is to get what they want. In film or on the street, people who describe themselves to you are lying. Here is the difference: In the bad film, the fellow says, "hello, Jack, I'm coming over to your home this evening because I need to get the money you borrowed from me." In the good film, he says, "where the hell were you yesterday?"

You don't have to narrate with the dialogue any more than you have to narrate with the pictures or the acting. The less you narrate, the more the audience is going to say, "wow. What the *heck* is happening here? What the *heck* is going to happen next . . . ?" Now, if you're telling the story with the pictures, then the dialogue is the sprinkles on top of the ice cream cone.

It's a gloss on what's happening. The story is being carried by the shots. Basically, the perfect movie doesn't have any dialogue. So you should always be striving to make a silent movie. If you don't, what will happen to you is the same thing that happened to the American film industry. Instead of writing the shot list, you'll have the student rise and say, "isn't that Mr. Smith? I think I'll get a retraction from him." Which is what happened to American films when sound came in, and they've gotten worse ever since.

If you can learn to tell a story, to break down a movie according to the shots and tell the story according to the theory of montage, then the dialogue, if it's good, will make the movie somewhat better; and if it's bad, will make the movie somewhat worse; but you'll still be telling the story *with the shots,* and they can take the brilliant dialogue out, if need be—as, in fact, they do when a film is subtitled or dubbed—and a great film, so treated, is injured hardly at all.

Now that we know what to tell the actors, we need an answer to the one question the crew will ask you again and again—"where do we put the camera?" The answer to this question is, "over there."

There are some directors who are visual masters—who bring to moviemaking a great visual acuity, a brilliant visual sense. I am not one of those people. So the answer I'm giving is the only answer I know. I happen to know a certain amount about the construction of a script, so that's what I'm telling you. The question is, "where do I put the camera?" That's the simple question, and the answer is, "over there in that place in which it will capture the uninflected shot necessary to move the story along."

"Yes, but," a lot of you are saying, "I know that the shot should be uninflected, but really since it's a scene about *respect* shouldn't we put the camera at a respectful angle?"

No; there is no such thing as "a respectful angle." Even if there *were,* you wouldn't want to put the camera there—if you did so, you wouldn't be letting the story *evolve.* It's like saying: "a naked man is walking down the street copulating with a whore while going to a whorehouse." Let him *get* to the whorehouse. Let each shot stand by itself. The answer to the question "where do you put the camera?" is the question "what's the shot of?"

That's my philosophy. I don't know better. If I knew a better answer to it, I would give it to you. If I knew a better answer to the shot, I would give it to you, but because I don't, I have to go back to step number one, which is "keep it simple, stupid, and don't violate those rules that you *do* know. If you don't know which rule applies, just don't muck up the more general rules."

I know it's a shot of *a guy walking down a hall.* I'm going to put the camera *somewhere.* Is one place better than another? Probably. Do I know which place is better than another? No? Then I'll let my subconscious pick one, and put the camera there.

Is there a better answer to the question? There may be, and the better answer may be this: in the storyboard for a movie or a scene, you may see a certain pattern developing, which might tell you something. Perhaps your task as a designer of shots is, after a point, that of a "decorator," quite frankly.

"What are the 'qualities' of the shot?" I don't happen to think that's the most important question in making a movie. I think it's an important question, but I don't think it's the most important question. When faced with the necessity of a particular election, I'm going to answer what I think is the most important question first, and then reason backward and answer the smaller question as best I can.

Where do you put the camera? We did our first movie and we had a bunch of shots with a hall here and a door there and a staircase there.

"Wouldn't it be nice," one might say, "if we could get this hall *here,* really around the corner from that door *there;* or to get that door *here* to *really be* the door that opens on the staircase to that door *there?*" So we could just move the camera from one to the next?

It took me a great deal of effort and still takes me a great deal and will continue to take me a great deal of effort to answer the question thusly: no, not only is it not important to have those objects literally contiguous; it is important to fight against this desire, because fighting it reinforces an understanding of the essential nature of film, which is that it is made of disparate shots, cut together. It's a *door,* it's a *hall,* it's a *blah-blah. Put* the camera "there" and photograph, *as simply as possible,* that object. If we don't understand that we both can and *must* cut the shots together, we are sneakily falling victim to the mistaken theory of the Steadicam. It might be nice to have these objects next to each other so as to avoid having to move the crew, but you don't get any sneaky artistic good out of literally having them next to each other. *You can cut the shots together.*

This relates to what I said about acting: if you can cut different pieces, different scenes together, different lines together, you don't have to have somebody in every shot with the same "continuous intention." The same "commitment to and understanding of the character." You don't need it.

The actor has to be performing a simple physical action for the space of ten seconds. It does not have to be part of the "performance of the film." Actors talk about the "arc of the film" or the "arc of the performance." It doesn't exist on stage. It's not there. The performance takes care of both. The "arc of the performance," the act of controlling, of doling out emotion here and withholding emotion there, just doesn't exist. It's like a passenger sticking his arms out of the airplane window and flapping them to make the plane more aerodynamic. This commitment to the arc of the film—it's ignorance on the part of the actor, ignorance of the essential nature of acting in film, which is that the performance will be created by the juxtaposition of simple, for the most part uninflected shots, and simple, uninflected physical actions.

The way to shoot the car crash is not to stick a guy in the middle of the street and run over him and keep the camera on. The way to shoot the car crash is to shoot the pedestrian walking across the street, shoot the shot of the onlooker whose head turns, shoot the shot of a man inside the car who looks up, shoot the shot of the guy's foot coming down on the brake pedal, and shoot the shot underneath the car with the set of legs lying at a strange angle (with thanks to Pudovkin, for the above). Cut them together, and the audience gets the idea: accident.

If that's the nature of film for the director, that's the nature of film for the actor too. Great actors understand this.

Humphrey Bogart told this story: When they were shooting *Casablanca* and S. Z. (Cuddles) Sakall or someone comes to him and says, "they want to play the 'Marseillaise,' what should we do?—the Nazis are here and we shouldn't be playing the 'Marseillaise,' " Humphrey Bogart just nods to the band, we cut to the band, and they start playing "bah-bah-bah-*bah*."

Someone asked what he did to make that beautiful scene work. He says, "they called me in one day, Michael Curtiz, the director, said, 'stand on the balcony over there, and when I say "action" take a beat and nod,' " which he did. That's great acting. Why? What more could he possibly have done? He was required to nod, he nodded. There you have it. The audience is terribly moved by his simple *restraint* in an emotional situation—and this is the essence of good theater: good theater is people doing extraordinarily moving tasks as simply as possible. Contemporary playwriting, filmmaking, and acting tend to offer us the reverse—people performing mundane and predictable actions in an overblown way. The good actor performs his tasks as simply and *as unemotionally* as possible. This lets the audience "get the idea"—just as the juxtaposition of uninflected images in service of a third idea creates the play in the mind of the audience.

Learn this, and go out and make the movie. You'll get someone who knows how to take a picture, or *you* learn how to take a picture; you get someone who knows how to light, or *you* learn how to light. There's no magic to it. Some people will be able to do some tasks better than others—depending upon the degree of their technical mastery and their aptitude for the task. Just like playing the piano. Anybody can learn how to play the piano. For some people it will be very, very difficult—but they can learn it. There's almost no one who can't learn to play the piano. There's a wide range in the middle, of people who can play the piano with various degrees of skill; a very, very narrow band at the top, of people who can play brilliantly and build upon a simple technical skill to create great art. The same thing is true of cinematography and sound mixing. Just technical skills. Directing is just a technical skill. Make your shot list.

# 5

# PIG—THE MOVIE

The questions that you want to ask as a director are the same questions you want to ask as a writer, the same questions you want to ask as an actor. "Why now?" "What happens if I don't?" Having discovered what is essential, you then know what to cut.

Why does the story start now? Why does Oedipus have to find out who his parents are? This is a trick question. The answer is this: he doesn't have to find out who his parents are. He has to cure the plague on Thebes. He discovers he, himself, is the cause of the plague on Thebes. His simple quest for external information led him on a journey, which resulted in his discovery. Oedipus is the model of all tragedy, according to Aristotle.

Dumbo has big ears; that's *his* problem. He was born with it. The problem gets worse, people make more and more fun of him. He has to try to learn to cure it. He meets little friends along the way who come to his aid in this classic myth. (The study of myth is very useful for directors.) Dumbo learns to fly; he develops a talent that he didn't realize he had and comes to this understanding about himself: that he's not worse than his fellows. He's perhaps not better, but he's different, and he has to be himself—when he realizes this, his journey is over. The problem of his big ears has been solved not by ear reduction but by self-discovery—and the story is over.

*Dumbo* is an example of a perfect movie. Cartoons are very good to watch—are much better to watch, for people who want to direct, than movies.

In the old cartoons, the artists realized the essence of the theory of montage, which is that they could do whatever the heck they wanted. It wasn't any more expensive to draw it from a high angle or from a long angle. They didn't have to keep the actors late to draw a hundred people rather than one person, or send out for that very expensive Chinese vase. Everything was based on the *imagination*. The shot we see in the film is the shot the artist saw in his imagination. So if you watch cartoons, you can learn a great deal about how to choose shots, how to tell the story in pictures, and how to cut.

Question: What starts the story *now?* Because if you don't know what starts the story, what's the impetus to start the story, then you have to rely on "back story" or history, all those dread terms that those swine out in Hollywood use to describe a process they not only do not understand but don't particularly care about. The story is not begun because the hero "suddenly gets an idea"——it is brought into being by a concrete external event: the plague on Thebes, the big ears, the death of Charles Foster Kane.

Thus you start the story in such a way that you bring along the audience. They are there *at the birth*. So they are going to want to know what happens next. "Once upon a time," for example, "there was a man who owned a farm" or "there were once three sisters." Just like a dirty joke. That's how the drama is structured——and this drama, like the dirty joke, is just a specialized form of fairy tale.

The fairy tale is a great teaching tool for directors. Fairy tales are told in the simplest of images and without elaboration, without an attempt to characterize. The characterization is left up to the audience.* In fairy tales, we see that it is simple to know when to begin and to know when to stop. And if one can apply those simple tests to the play as a whole, one can apply them to the scene, which is only a small play, and to the beat, which is only . . . et cetera.

"Once there was a farmer who wanted to sell his pig." How do I know when I'm finished? When the pig's sold, or when the farmer discovers that he cannot sell the pig——when the end of that syllogism has come to pass.

Now, not only do I know when to start and when I want to stop, but I also know what to keep in and what to throw out. The farmer's interesting encounter with a female swineherd, which has nothing to do with selling the pig, probably shouldn't

*Bettelheim, *The Uses of Enchantment.*

be in the movie. In plotting a film, one can also ask: "what am I missing here?" Am I going from the beginning to the end in a logical progression? And if not, what missing term will render the progression logical?

Here's a story: "once there was a farmer who wanted to sell a pig." Now, how do you open the film? What are the shots? How do you make up your shot list?

STUDENT:    You establish a good farm.

MAMET:     Why do you have to establish a good farm? Everybody in Hollywood always whines, "but we won't know where we *are* . . ." But I put it to you, ladies and gentlemen, how often in the thousands of movies that we've all seen has anyone said, "hey, wait a second, I don't know where I am"? In fact, quite the contrary is true. You come to a movie in the middle, turn on the TV in the middle, look at a tape in the middle, you know exactly what's happening, always, immediately. You are interested in it because you want to know what's going on. That's what interests you. What would be better than an establishing shot of a farm? What will answer the question "why now?"

STUDENT:    The reason he has to sell his pig?

MAMET:     The reason he has to sell his pig. What's his reason? The answer will lead us to a very specific beginning. A beginning specific to *this film*—rather than one specific to *a* film. "Once there was a farmer who wanted to sell his pig" leads us to "once there was a farmer who *had* to sell his pig." You will find that the study of semantics, which is the study of how words influence thought and action, will help you immensely as a director. Notice the difference in those two beginnings: they lead you down very divergent trains of thought. They will change the words you use to tell your ideas to the actors. It's very, very important to be concise. Okay: "once there was a farmer who had to sell his pig."

STUDENT: A wide shot of pigs in a pasture. And then the farmer walking across the pasture. The next shot is a For Sale sign that he is hammering.

MAMET: Into his pig?

STUDENT: Into a post.

MAMET: Uh huh. Exposition in film is like exposition in any art form. If you explain the joke's punch line, the audience might understand it, but they won't laugh. The real art, the essential art in choosing the shots, is not so much to make the audience understand as to invest yourself in the clear telling of the story. You aren't smarter than *they* are. *They*'re smarter than *you* are. *You* understand the story as well as you possibly can, and then they will too. Putting up a sign is an easy way out. That's not *always* bad per se, but I think we can do better. We can ask *what the character is doing,* but better to ask *what is the meaning of this scene?* (To help understand this distinction, may I recommend the "Analysis" chapter of *A Practical Handbook for the Actor,* Bruder, Cohn, Olnek, et al.)

Literally, on the page, as it is written, the farmer has to sell his pig. What does this mean in this scene? The *essence* of having to sell one's pig could be many different things. The essence could be, a man fell on hard times. The essence could be, a man had to leave his ancestral home. A man had to take leave of his best friend.

STUDENT: A man had to do his duty.

STUDENT: A man had too many pigs.

MAMET: Well, yes. But you're thinking on a different level of abstraction. The point is not the pigs, right? The point is *what does the pig mean to the man?* A man's business, for example? What might be the meaning of that? A man's business grew too fast for him. What you want to dramatize is not the *surface,* "a man needs to sell his pig," but the *essence*—what selling the pig means in *this* story.

Why does he need to sell the pig? The more specifically you think about the nature of the story, the more you can think of the essence of the scene rather than the appearance of the scene, then the easier it will be to find the images. It's a lot easier to find specific images for "a man fell on reduced circumstances" than for "once there was a man who had to sell a pig."

Jung wrote that one can't stand aloof from the

images, the stories, of the person who's being analyzed. One has to enter into them.

If you enter into them, they'll mean something to you. If you don't enter into them, then your subconscious will never work. You'll never come up with anything that the audience couldn't have thought of better at home.

It's like the actor who goes home and figures out what the performance is supposed to mean, then shows up on the stage and does *that* performance. The audience will probably understand this actor, and his performance, but they won't care.*

"Pig for Sale." Why? The problem starts now. The picture starts with the inception or the discovery of the problem. Most movies start thusly: "honey, is that damn pig, which we can ill afford to keep, still eating up the last groceries in the

---

*Stanislavsky said that there are three types of actors. The first presents a ritualized and superficial version of human behavior, this version coming from his observation of other bad actors. This actor will give the audience a stock rendition of "love," "anger," or whatever emotion seems to be called for by the text. The second actor sits with the script and comes up with his *own* unique and interesting version of the behavior supposedly called for by the scene, and he comes to the set or stage to present *that*. The third, called the "organic" actor by Stanislavsky, realizes that *no* behavior or emotion is called for by the text—that only *action* is called for by the text—and he comes to the set or stage armed only with his analysis of the scene and prepared to act moment-to-moment, based on what occurs in the performance . . . to deny nothing and *to invent nothing*. This last, organic actor is the artist with whom the director wants to work. He is also the artist we most admire on stage and in films. *Curiously,* he is not the artist most usually

house?" The real artistry of the film director is to learn to do without the exposition; and, so, involve the audience. Let's come up with some dramatic shot lists that are going to communicate the idea "why now?"

STUDENT:   The letter from the bank arrives?

MAMET:   Let's stay away from that.

STUDENT:   Start in a graveyard, and the farmer is at the grave, and the next shot would be the house and it's nearly deserted and there's no food in the cupboard.

MAMET:   When we see the empty cupboard, we might wonder, why don't they just kill the pig? Here's a different story: A small child is dressed in rags and playing in the yard and then a shot of the pig jumping over the fence and attacking the child. Eh? Kid playing in the yard—she sees something, starts to run away. Second shot, a pig jumps into the thing, squeak, squeak, squeak, squeak, squeak; and the third shot is the farmer walking down the

---

denominated the *great* actor. Over the years, I have observed that there are two subdivisions of the thespian's art: one is called Acting, and the other is called Great Acting; and that, universally, those who are known as the Great Actors, the Premier Actors of their age, fall into the second of Stanislavsky's categories. They bring to the stage and screen an intellectual pomposity. The audience calls them Great, I think, because it wants to identify with them—with the *actors,* that is, not with the characters the actors portray. The audience wants to identify with these actors because they seem empowered to behave arrogantly in a protected setting. On the other hand, look at the old character actors and comedians: Harry Carey, H. B. Warner, Edward Arnold, William Demarest; look at Thelma Ritter, Mary Astor, Celia Johnson. *Those* people could *act.*

road with the pig. Does that tell you a story? Yes.

But how can we do it without showing the pig mauling the child? We don't want to show the pig mauling the child, because that has one of two results. Every time you show the audience something that is "real," they think one of two things: (1) "oh, dash it all, that's fake" or (2) "oh my God, that's *real!*" Each one of these takes the audience away from the story you're telling,* and neither one is better than the other. "Oh, he's not really copulating with her" or "oh my God, he's really copulating with her!" Both lose the audience. If we *suggest* the idea, we can shoot it better than if we *show* it.

What about we cut from kid playing in the yard to mom's in the kitchen, she snaps around, and then she's running out, she grabs a broom, for example. Third shot is dad walking the pig out of the barn. He's on the road, we see him going on past the gate. He's obviously going to get rid of the pig.

STUDENT: But he could just shoot the pig. Don't we have to show the empty cupboard to show why he has to sell the pig?

MAMET: If you try to narrate the fact that the family is on the brink of poverty, you split your focus. You split it between (1) "I need the money" and (2) "the pig just attacked my daughter." Now the guy has two

---

*This is the meaning of the concept "violating the aesthetic distance."

reasons to sell the pig, which is not as good as one reason to sell the pig. Two reasons are equal to no reasons—it's like saying: "I was late because the bus drivers are on strike and my aunt fell downstairs."

And so now, what's the idea: once upon a time, *a man had to sell a dangerous pig.*

STUDENT:  The first shot is the child playing in the yard.

STUDENT:  The second shot is the pig eyeing her.

STUDENT:  Cut to mom in the kitchen.

MAMET:   She hears something, she turns, she picks up a broom and runs out of the house. Cut to a shot of the farmer leading the pig down the road. Okay.

Here's another possibility. There's an interior of a barn. It's a shot of the door. Door opens, here comes a farmer in work clothes. He comes in and lays down his hoe, picks up a lantern and lights it. Now he turns, and there's a tracking shot of him walking past a row of empty pens to one pen that has a pig in it. He puts the lantern on the ledge. He reaches down and takes out a small trough and puts it in front of the pig. Then he comes up and empties a sack of grain into the trough. He turns the sack upside down and empties it. Then cut back to the shot of the trough, and only two or three kernels fall into it. Then next day—that is, *exterior day,* which shows the audience that *time has passed.* We know the barn sequence was at night—it involved lighting a lantern. This is a shot of an exterior, and it is day. It may be picayune to suggest that a filmscript not contain the description "the next day"—but as the audience can only determine that it *is* "the next day" from that which they see on the screen, perhaps it would be a salutary habit only to *describe* those things that the audience is going to see on the screen. The shot of the farmer leading the pig down the road: how does that work?

STUDENT: We're not worrying about the baby anymore.

MAMET: That's right. It's a different story. One is the idea of a man *getting rid of danger*, a man *eradicating danger*. The other is a man *brought to straitened circumstances*. Yeah, you're right. I like the dangerous pig more. How do we know when that story is over?

STUDENT: He sells it or he doesn't.

MAMET: So what happens now? "John," the pig's owner, is walking down along the road with the pig, when he comes to a crossroads, and as we say in Chicago, he sees a prosperous-looking man walking down the road. They enter into a conversation, and John convinces the man to buy his pig. Just as the deal is about to be concluded, however, what happens?

STUDENT: The pig bites the man.

MAMET: We said the essence of the scene was the man wants to divest himself of the pig. He's offered a perfect opportunity to sell the pig. Great, we didn't expect it, we thought we were going to have to go all the darned way to town and have to take the bus home, with nothing to read. Now, out of nowhere, comes this guy, a buyer, a perfect opportunity presents itself, and what happens? The pig, the dangerous pig, bites the guy. Now, what's this beat about?

STUDENT: *Failed attempt.*

MAMET: No, let's describe the beat as a step on the road to the objective of the scene, which is to divest oneself of a dangerous commodity. You might say, *capitalizing on a golden opportunity.* That is the *active* thrust of the beat. "Failed attempt" is just the result.

The great thing about this method is this: what did we say the film was about? *A man had to rid his house of danger. That*'s what you go out to film. *It doesn't matter* that all your cinematographers and assistant directors and producers are pleading with you to show more of the farm. You'll say to them, "why? It's not a movie about a farm. You want to see a movie about a farm? Great. You know? Go see a travelogue. Go look at a map. This is a movie about a man who has to rid his house of danger. Let's make *this* movie. The audience knows what a farm looks like or they don't. That's their lookout. Let's respect their privacy." So, *a man tries to capitalize on a golden opportunity.*

STUDENT: Well, we could start with him walking with the pig, and on the roadside, fixing a broken cart wheel, he sees another farmer. And he goes over and takes the initiative to talk to that man.

MAMET: Stay with the shots: our guy walking down the road. He stops because he sees something. Come to his point of view, a cart with a broken wheel, two pigs in the back, and a prosperous farmer is fixing the cart wheel. Now, what would we like to include?

To keep the idea of *capitalize,* what about if he does something with the pig?

STUDENT: He might walk differently, knowing he was going to sell the pig.

MAMET: The idea is *capitalize.* The verb is not *to make a sale* but *to capitalize.*

STUDENT: He can spruce up the pig.

MAMET: The shot is: he takes out a handkerchief and wipes off the pig's face. He wants to sell the pig.

STUDENT: He might take the handkerchief and put it around the pig's neck.

MAMET: I like this handkerchief. Let's think of something else. How else could he capitalize? He wipes the pig's face off and he ties the thing around the pig and he walks over to the guy. What's going to happen now?

STUDENT: Maybe he would help the guy fix the cart wheel. That way he would get into his confidence.

MAMET: He could do that. That would help him capitalize. *Good.*

STUDENT: When he helps the guy, that would make his sale easier.

MAMET: Yes. We got the shot of him sprucing up the pig, now a shot of him as he leads the pig over to the farmer, who's just pulling the cart out, maybe helps him push the cart the last inch up the road, and the shot of these two guys talking for a couple of seconds. The new farmer looks down at the pig, looks up at the guy, they talk, the new guy reaches in his pocket, gives our guy some money. It doesn't have to be more intricate than that. Does that tell the story?

Or else you don't have him putting the hand in the pocket. You have the two guys talking, blah-blah-blah . . .

STUDENT: . . . and the shot of that pig, with the same look he had before he attacked the little girl.

MAMET: Exactly so. We have the two guys talking, and they shake hands. Now we have a shot of the new farmer picking the old pig up and putting the pig inside his cart. It's an open cart, so we can have a shot of the pig in the cart, extreme close-up of the pig. We cut to the pig's point of view, through the bars, of the two guys talking. While the new farmer puts his hand in his pocket for money, we cut to the shot of . . .

STUDENT: . . . the pig jumping out of the cart, and the next shot is *our* farmer walking down the road with the pig.

MAMET: Great. Now we are really telling the story of "once there was a farmer who tried everything he could to sell a dangerous pig."

So now our guy is back to walking down the road with the pig. What's the next interchange going to be? Where's he going to go? Anybody? Let's make sure we follow the rule against circularity. Don't do the same thing twice. This *circularity*, or repetition of the same incident in different guises, is antithetical to the dramatic form. It is the signature of both the *epic* and the *autobiography*, and the reason both are adapted into drama with much difficulty and little success.

STUDENT: The slaughterhouse.

MAMET: We're going to go to the slaughterhouse next. All right. But before we get there, we want to move the story along. Why was it a golden opportunity when he saw the farmer on the road?

STUDENT: Because he didn't have to travel.

MAMET: So because he blew that golden opportunity, *now* what?

STUDENT: He has to go all the way into town, after all.

MAMET: And with what time-honored convention of cinema do we dramatize that?

STUDENT: It's night, and it used to be day . . . ?

MAMET: It's night, and we are at the slaughterhouse. The dark, inky, Egyptian blackness of night has fallen as only it knows how to fall. Unencumbered by the roseate glow of the mercury vapor lamps of the city streets, reflected by the trapped smog of the inversion layer caused by those internal combustion engines so favored by today's urban men and women as a means of powering those machines designed and appointed for their conveyance. Night, I say again, *night* has fallen. One half of that circularity, in sum, that never-ending round of day-and-night. Night: for some a time of sleep, while for others a time of wakefulness, as in the case of our farmer. Night has fallen.

Now, our farmer walks into town, walks wearily into town, it being night, and walks up to the slaughterhouse. Anybody?

STUDENT: What if it's locked?

MAMET: The slaughterhouse is locked, and then what? Do it in shots.

STUDENT: Shot of the road at night with the farmer and pig. Another shot of the slaughterhouse. Takes the pig over there. Shot of the farmer at the slaughterhouse door, which is locked.

MAMET: Yes. What idea do we seem to be dramatizing here?

STUDENT: Last chance to sell the pig?

MAMET: Let's call this beat *the end of the weary quest*. It's not that it's his last chance; it's that the story is over. Now we're getting good luck as the residue of good design, we're getting some extra mileage out of having been assiduous and following the form. What's the extra mileage? It's night because it took him a long time to get to the slaughterhouse. It took him a long time because he didn't get a ride on the truck. He didn't get a ride because the pig bit the driver. That same dangerous pig about whom we are now composing a story—so that even the *night* is a function of the throughline. The extra mileage is that the slaughterhouse is locked. Now we have a raking shot from around the corner of the front of the slaughterhouse, and we see that the light is on, and we see in the office, the little office, we see the light go off. A guy comes out the office door, turns the key, and walks off screen left, as the farmer comes up from the right and tries the door. So it's *the end of the weary quest.*

STUDENT: How do we know it's a slaughterhouse?

MAMET: How do we know it's a slaughterhouse? There's a big pen full of pigs behind it. We don't have to know it's a slaughterhouse. We have to know it's *where he wants to go.* It's the end of the quest. There's a building with a pen with a lot of pigs in it, and he's walking toward it.

"The end of the quest" does not, however, mean the end of the story. *End of the weary quest* is only the title of this *beat.* Every turn takes us to the next. That's why it's a good story. Oedipus wants to end the plague. He finds that this plague hit because somebody killed his father, and he finds that he's the guy. Any good drama takes us deeper and deeper to a resolution that is both surprising and inevitable. It's like Turkish taffy; it always tastes good and it always sticks to your teeth.

STUDENT: Do you need the guy leaving the slaughterhouse?

MAMET: I think so. But it's the same question as "where do you put the camera?" At some point, you, the director, are going to make some decisions, which may seem arbitrary but which in fact may be based on a continually emerging aesthetic understanding of the story. My answer to your question is: "I think so." *End of the weary quest.*

What tool are we going to use to help us determine what happens next?

STUDENT: The *throughline*.

MAMET: And we know the throughline is he wants *to rid himself of a dangerous pig.*

STUDENT: So he sits down and waits.

MAMET: He could sit down and wait at the slaughterhouse.

STUDENT: He could tie up the pig at the slaughterhouse and go down the block to the bar. Sits down and has a drink, and the farmer from before comes in and starts a fight. We come back to the pig, he's tugging on the rope and he breaks free and runs into the bar and saves our guy.

MAMET: Now we get a little bit of extra bang for our buck! We got interested in our story and the quiddities and oddities of the story; and what suggested itself was a possible ending to our story. And the reason that we laugh at our ending is it contains the two essential elements that we learned of from Aristotle, *surprise* and *inevitability.*

Aristotle uses rather different words, as he's talking about tragedy rather than drama: he calls the two fear and pity. Pity because of the fate of the poor guy who got himself in such a jam; and fear because, in identifying with the hero, we see that it could also happen to us.

The reason we identify is that the writer left out the narration. We only saw the story.

We can identify with the pursuit of a goal. It's much easier to identify with that than with "character traits."

Most movies are written, "he's the wacky kind of guy who . . ." But then we can't identify with that person. We don't see ourselves in him because we aren't being shown his struggle but instead are shown those idiosyncrasies that *divide* us from him. His "knowledge of karate," his wacky habit of yodeling to call his dogs, his peculiar partiality to antique cars . . . how interesting. It's a good thing that the people in Hollywood have no souls, so that they don't have to suffer through the lives they lead. Who would like to suggest another ending?

STUDENT: I was just thinking that perhaps the pig has to fight one more person.

MAMET: As Leadbelly says about the blues, he says in the first verse use a knife to cut bread, and in the second verse use a knife to shave, and in the third verse use it to kill your unfaithful girlfriend. It's the same knife, but the stakes change, which is exactly the way a play or movie is structured. You don't want to use the knife in the first verse to cut bread and in the second verse use it to cut cheese. We already know it can cut bread. What *else* can it do?

STUDENT: But shouldn't we elaborate on the pig's danger somehow, at this point, to raise the stakes?

MAMET:      We don't have to get him in trouble. We've got to
            get him *out* of trouble. Remember, our task is not
            to create chaos but rather to create order out of a
            situation that has become chaotic. We don't have
            to worry about making it interesting; all we have
            to worry about is getting rid of the pig.

            Let's complete this story in a happy, peppy man-
            ner that is both surprising and inevitable or, at the
            very least, pleasing, or, at the very, *very* least, in-
            ternally consistent. We're sitting on the steps with
            the pig. It's nighttime. The slaughterhouse is locked.

STUDENT:    Well, the next shot is it's daylight and there's a guy
            walking up the steps to open up the front door of
            the slaughterhouse and can you guess what's going
            to happen then? He's going to sell the pig.

MAMET:      And then the movie's over. Okay.

STUDENT:    How about: it's morning, he wakes up, he thinks
            something is missing or he feels for his wallet and
            it's gone. Then we cut to the pig sitting there peace-
            fully and then another shot, a guy lying there dead
            with our guy's wallet in his hand. The pig saved his
            wallet.

MAMET:      So the pig redeems himself and he can set the pig
            free. *Setting the pig free* fulfills his original purpose,
            doesn't it? If the original purpose is to rid himself
            of danger.

STUDENT:    Why didn't he set the pig free before?

MAMET:      All right. Good. You have found a very important
            logical *lacuna* in our film. He is trying, throughout,

*to rid himself of danger.* After the first sequence, when the pig attacks the little girl, we, as you point out, need a *second* sequence, which we might call "the easy solution to a difficult problem." In this sequence, the farmer is leading the pig away. Shot of the pig, abandoned, on a hillside. Shot, pig's point of view, of the farmer walking away.

Shot of the farmer approaching his house. The farmer stops. Shot, his point of view, of the pig, back in his appointed stall. And then we resume the story, and the next sequence, after "The Easy Solution," is "Capitalizing on a Golden Opportunity."

Good. I think this discovery makes it a better movie. By the way, I have always found that these piddling points inevitably reveal most important information when they are explored. They are, I think, like the minor or half-forgotten points in dreams. One is tempted to brush past them and think of them as unimportant. But *no* step in the logical progression is unimportant. And I know, from my own experience, that persistence in these "small" points will be rewarded.

Here's another possible ending. It's dawn. Your sound department is torturing you to okay the inclusion of the sound of birds chirping, ladies and gentlemen. Oh, well. You see the same guy from the office open up the slaughterhouse and see the pig. He opens up and leads the pig into the pen.

Our guy wakes up, there's no pig. He goes in, he wants his pig. The owner says, "how am I going to know what pig is yours, bobbity, bobbity, bobbity." Our man is obstreperous. The owner of the slaughterhouse gets in a fight with our farmer and is going to brain him to get him to stop bothering him about the pig. We cut to a shot of the pig, our proverbial pig shot, looking back through the fence at our guy. We know it's *our* pig because it's wearing the handkerchief it acquired in the "golden opportunity" beat, *hein*? Next we have a shot of the slaughterhouse owner turning, and then a shot of our guy, walking back down along the road with the pig. Close-up: our guy stops, turns.

Angle: the pig, who is looking back down the road. Hold on this. The farmer starts walking the pig back in the direction the pig is looking.

Cut to our proverbial pig shot, our pig looking at something. Shot of our farmer paying some money to the slaughterhouse owner. Back to the pig shot, back to the slaughterhouse owner taking the money, slaughterhouse owner moving gingerly past our pig.

Our pig looking through the bars. Shot, his point of view: the slaughterhouse owner entering a pen in which is one single pig. He starts to lead this pig out.

Now. Final sequence. Our farmer walking down the road with *two* pigs. Shot of the farmhouse. The wife comes out. Shot, her point of view: our farmer leading home the two pigs. Shot of the barnyard fence. The gate is swung open, the two pigs enter. Shot of the farmer looking on. Shot of the two pigs kissing. Fade out, fade in. Shot of a pig suckling many little piglets. Shot of "our" pig, with the handkerchief around his neck, riding the little girl around on his back. Shot of our farmer looking on. What a pig. That's the movie, perhaps. He solved his problem. He didn't get rid of the pig, he got rid of the danger. Now, you can look back over the shot list and ask, "what have I left out?" As you have devoted yourself consciously, honestly, and gently to the story, you will have created a certificate of deposit, if you will, in your subconscious, on which you can draw for simple answers to the question of "where shall I put the camera?"—such questions also being aided by your reference to your list of objectives: a man tries to rid himself of danger, a man takes the easy solution to a difficult problem, a man tries to capitalize on a golden opportunity, a man comes to the end of a long quest, a man tries to regain possession, a man rewards a good deed. That is the story the director must tell— the internal story of the hero's persistence in a difficult world. Anybody with a Brownie can take a picture of a "pig."

# 6

## CONCLUSION

It's always up to you to decide whether you are going to tell the story through a juxtaposition of shots or whether you are not. It's *not* always up to you to decide whether or not that process is going to be interesting. Any real technique is going to be based on things within your control. Anything that is not based on things within your control is not a real technique. We would like to learn a technique of directing and analyzing as concrete as that of the shoemaker. The shoemaker will not say when the harness breaks, "golly, you know, I did it in the most interesting way I knew how!" Stanislavsky was once having dinner with a steamboat captain on the Volga River and Stanislavsky said, "how is it that among all the major and minor paths of the Volga River, which are so many and so dangerous, you manage to always steer the boat safely?" And the captain said, "I stick to the channel; it's marked." And the same thing is true here.

How is it that, given the many, many ways one might direct a movie, one might always be able, with economy, and perhaps a certain amount of grace, to tell the story? The answer is: "stick to the channel; it's marked." The channel is the super-objective of the hero, and the marker buoys are the small objectives of each scene and the smaller objectives of each beat, and the smallest unit of all, which is the shot.

The shots are all you have. That's it. Your choice of the shots is all you have. It's what the movie is going to be made up of. *You can't make it more interesting when you get to the editing room.* And also you can't rely on the actors to take up the slack. You can't rely on them to "make it more interesting." That's not their job either. You want them to be as simple as you are in your choice of the shots.

If you're correct in the small things, the smallest of which in this case is the choice of a single uninflected shot, then you will be correct in the larger things. And then your film will be as correct and as ordered and as well-intentioned as *you* are. It can never be more so, but it can be less so if you desire to manipulate the material, or hope that God will intervene and save you, which is what most people mean when they talk about "talent."

You might want the shoemakers' elves to save you, but how wonderful it is not to *need* the elves to save you. Especially under conditions of great stress, you have to know your trade. And there is a trade to screenwriting and there is a trade to directing a movie. They're very much the same trade. If you pay the price, you can learn that trade. If you persevere, that analytical method of thinking will become easier for you. The problems of the individual films will not get easier—they only get easier for hacks. The task is always the same. Stick with it until you solve it. It's not your job to make it pretty. It will be as pretty or unpretty as God intended. It's your job to make it correct according to your first principles.

We, just like the protagonists in our movies, have a task. In completing the task, we have to go from one thing to the next as logically as possible. Our work is like mountain climbing. It's frightening sometimes and it's usually arduous, but we don't have to climb the whole mountain all at once. All we have to do is make a foothold here, figure out what that beat is or what that shot is or what that scene is; and when we're completely secure here, *reach* until we get the next foothold that is absolutely secure. Dramatic analysis is a bit like plotting out a compass course over rough territory. When we get lost, or get confused, terrified, tired, frightened, all of which will happen to you if you do get the chance to direct a movie, all we have to do is refer to our map and compass. The analysis is not the movie, any more than the map is the terrain—but the right compass and analysis will enable you to navigate both.

The more time you have invested, and the more of yourself you have invested in the plan, the more secure you will feel in the face of terror, loneliness, or the unfeeling or ignorant comments of those from whom you are asking a whole bunch of money or indulgence.

Someone once asked Daniel Boone if he had ever been lost.

He replied, "I was never lost, but I was once a mite bewildered for three days."

It's good, as the Stoics tell us, to have tools that are simple to understand and of a very limited number—so that we may locate and employ them on a moment's notice. I think the essential tools in any worthwhile endeavor are incredibly simple. And very difficult to master. The task of any artist is not to learn many, many techniques but to learn the most simple technique perfectly. In doing so, Stanislavsky told us, the difficult will become easy and the easy habitual, so that the habitual may become beautiful.

It is the pursuit of an *ideal* that is important. This pursuit will lead to a greater possibility of the unconscious asserting itself, which is to say, the greater possibility of beauty in your work. The Navahos, I am told, used to weave flaws into their blankets to let the devils out.

Some contemporary artist said, "well, we don't have to weave in the flaws. We can try to weave perfectly. God will see that there're enough flaws in them anyway; that's human nature."

The application of these principles, in my experience, will help you to weave as perfectly as is humanly possible—which is to say not very perfectly at all.

Keep giving yourself over to the simple task. This dedication will give you great satisfaction. The very fact that you have forsworn the Cult of Self for a little while—the cult of how interesting you and your consciousness are—will communicate itself to the audience. And they will be appreciative in the extreme and give you the benefit of every doubt.

Is it possible to "do everything right" and still come up with a bad movie? To "do everything right" means to progress according to philosophically correct principles step by step such that your evaluation of your own effort is honest and you are happy that you have fulfilled the specific task at hand. Is it possible to do that and come up with a bad movie? What's the answer to that? Well, it depends on your definition of bad. Once again, a tool that the Stoics would advise us to use is this: if, before going into battle, you asked an omen of the gods and they told you that you were about to lose, would you not be bound to fight in any case?

It's not up to you to say whether the movie is going to be "good" or "bad"; it's only up to you to do your job as well as you can, and when you're done, then you can go home. This is exactly the same principle as the *throughline*. Understand your specific task, work until it's done, and then stop.

# FOR THE BEST IN PAPERBACKS, LOOK FOR THE

In every corner of the world, on every subject under the sun, Penguin represents quality and variety—the very best in publishing today.

For complete information about books available from Penguin—including Puffins, Penguin Classics, and Compass—and how to order them, write to us at the appropriate address below. Please note that for copyright reasons the selection of books varies from country to country.

**In the United Kingdom:** Please write to *Dept. EP, Penguin Books Ltd, Bath Road, Harmondsworth, West Drayton, Middlesex UB7 0DA.*

**In the United States:** Please write to *Penguin Putnam Inc., P.O. Box 12289 Dept. B, Newark, New Jersey 07101-5289* or call 1-800-788-6262.

**In Canada:** Please write to *Penguin Books Canada Ltd, 10 Alcorn Avenue, Suite 300, Toronto, Ontario M4V 3B2.*

**In Australia:** Please write to *Penguin Books Australia Ltd, P.O. Box 257, Ringwood, Victoria 3134.*

**In New Zealand:** Please write to *Penguin Books (NZ) Ltd, Private Bag 102902, North Shore Mail Centre, Auckland 10.*

**In India:** Please write to *Penguin Books India Pvt Ltd, 11 Panchsheel Shopping Centre, Panchsheel Park, New Delhi 110 017.*

**In the Netherlands:** Please write to *Penguin Books Netherlands bv, Postbus 3507, NL-1001 AH Amsterdam.*

**In Germany:** Please write to *Penguin Books Deutschland GmbH, Metzlerstrasse 26, 60594 Frankfurt am Main.*

**In Spain:** Please write to *Penguin Books S. A., Bravo Murillo 19, 1° B, 28015 Madrid.*

**In Italy:** Please write to *Penguin Italia s.r.l., Via Benedetto Croce 2, 20094 Corsico, Milano.*

**In France:** Please write to *Penguin France, Le Carré Wilson, 62 rue Benjamin Baillaud, 31500 Toulouse.*

**In Japan:** Please write to *Penguin Books Japan Ltd, Kaneko Building, 2-3-25 Koraku, Bunkyo-Ku, Tokyo 112.*

**In South Africa:** Please write to *Penguin Books South Africa (Pty) Ltd, Private Bag X14, Parkview, 2122 Johannesburg.*